Rare Support Materials for Manuscripts and their Conservation

The National Mission for Manuscripts was established in February 2003 by the Government of India with Indira Gandhi National Centre for the Arts (IGNCA) as the nodal agency. At present it is a part of IGNCA.

Its purpose is to locate, document, preserve and disseminate the knowledge content of Indian manuscripts. The Mission, through its nationwide network and documentation efforts, is engaged in preserving the physical form and rendering accessible India's textual heritage, seeking to link the knowledge of the past with the future.

Saṁrakṣikā (conservation related seminar and workshop) series is one of various outreach programmes conducted by the Mission. The first volume of Saṁrakṣikā, published in 2006, dealt with Indigenous Methods of Preservation and Conservation of Manuscripts. The present volume is the culmination of the lectures during a number of workshops on 'Rare Support Materials for Manuscripts and their Conservation'. They provide valuable information on techniques and science of conservation of writing materials.

The contributors are listed in alphabetic order: Achal Pandya, B.V. Kharbade, D.D.N. Singh, D.G. Suryawanshi, K.K. Gupta, Samiran Boruah and V. Jeyaraj.

Saṁrakṣikā Series
No. 2

The Samrakṣikā Series is aimed at publishing the papers presented by the experts in the conservation related seminars and workshops organized by the National Mission for Manuscripts, IGNCA. The seminars provide an interactive forum for experts to present to the interested audience ideas related to the conservation of manuscripts.

In keeping with the title, this Samrakṣikā (conservation) series deals primarily with the techniques of conservation of rare support materials used for the writing. The Series contains research papers of distinguished people who are specialized in the related field.

Rare Support Materials for Manuscripts and their Conservation

Edited by

K.K. Gupta

National Mission for Manuscripts

Indira Gandhi National Centre for the Arts

DEV BOOKS

Published by:
National Mission for Manuscripts
Indira Gandhi National Centre for the Arts
5, Rajendra Prasad Road
New Delhi 110 001
Phone: 91 11 2307 3387
e-mail: directornamami@nic.in
website: www.namami.nic.in

and Co-published by:

DEV BOOKS

2nd Floor, Prakash Deep,
4735/22, Ansari Road,
Darya Ganj,
New Delhi-110002
Phone : 9810236140
e-mail: devbooks@hotmail.com
website: www.devbooks.co.in

ISBN 81–904029–2–7 (vol. II)
First published 2010

Contents

Preface

THE STUDY OF writing in India is mainly concerned with two periods separated from each other by about two thousand years. The first period involves the early Indus Valley Civilization of the third millenium BC. We have evidence of written communication in the Indus Valley but these symbols have not yet been deciphered, and therefore, it is difficult to posit that they are alphabets. The second period involves what is generally considered the beginning of Indic writing proper in the fifth century BC, although the earliest long decuments—the Ashokan inscriptions—belong to the third century BC.

Manuscripts are handwritten documents of yesteryears. The National Mission for Manuscripts, established in February 2003 by the Government of India has the mandate of documenting, protecting and making accessible the rich manuscript heritage of India.

The vast richness and diversity of Indian manuscripts owes its origin to the fact that these manuscripts are composed in different languages and are written in various scripts. Some of them have also been illustrated to give a visual dimension to the content. These manuscripts are spread over a number of disciplines. We come across old manuscripts dealing with philosophy, literature, culture, politics, architecture, science and medicine. People of ancient times used to take a good care of the manuscripts in order to protect them for posterity so that the future generations are benefitted by the knowledge contained therein. Thus the most important objective of the Mission is to spread public awareness about the immense wealth of manuscripts as important historical sources, as well as to facilitate their conservation and preservation. We cannot afford to lose the manuscripts, the vehicle of cultural legacy and records of the past.

Manuscripts are scattered in known and unknown private and public collections across the country. The National Mission for Manuscripts from its inception has placed great emphasis on *conservation* of the vast number of important manuscripts in the country. In order to fulfil its objectives, the Mission has established Manuscript Resource Centres and Manuscript Conservation Centres in different regions of India.

In an attempt to connect the present with India's knowledge of the past stored in the manuscripts, the Mission started, along with other outreach programmes, *Saṁrakṣikā* (Conservation related seminar and workshop) series. The first Saṁrakṣikā seminar was on '*Indigenous Methods of Preservation and Conservation of Manuscripts*'. The first volume of Saṁrakṣikā, published in 2006, contained the proceedings of the seminars on the same topic presented by the experts in their respective fields.

The second volume of Saṁrakṣikā series comprises the papers of the workshops on '*Conservation of Rare Manuscript Support Materials*'. In this volume, conservation experts have shared their experiences on conservation technique of different manuscript materials like ivory, sanchipat, kadita, parchment, metal and palmleaf. Since a manuscript is any written document that is put down by hand, materials like clay tablet, stone, metal, bark, animal skin, bone, wood, ivory, conchshell, cloth, papyrus (a type of pulp of a reed), leaf, bamboo, etc., were used for this purpose. Stone, metal, etc. as they are not easily damaged in course of time, were used for important and more permanent documents by kings and governments. On the contrary manuscripts on palmleaves and other such materials, though not so longlasting, were popular as they were affordable to common man, could be handled easily and furthermore, had the advantage of easy transportation.

We hope that this book will be useful to the manuscript collectors and conservators and will accomplish the specific purpose of the workshop for which it was organized by the Mission.

SANGHAMITRA BASU

January, 2010
New Delhi.

Introduction

Writing Materials have played a very important role in the development of cultures. Though, today the paper is the most prominent support material used for writing manuscripts, many important manuscripts have been written on the materials other than paper. Paper was invented in 105 AD in China and reached India in about eleventh century. Before the invention of paper and even after, some other materials such as parchment, stone, palm leaf and birch bark were used as writing surface for manuscripts,

National Mission for Manuscripts (NMM) has found in its survey that there are more than five million manuscripts scattered in several repositories of manuscripts all over the country. These manuscripts are important as regards the historicity of their origin in its physical form, as well as the knowledge they contain. The digitization of these manuscripts is not enough as it can only preserve the knowledge contained in them. Conservation of the physical form of the manuscripts is as important as the preservation of this knowledge. NMM, therefore, took action to organize seminars and workshops on conservation of manuscripts. The Mission also realized that disseminating only the knowledge of conservation of paper manuscripts fulfils its function only partially, and it is important that the owners, custodians and caretakers of the manuscripts be educated in care and conservation of manuscripts on materials other than paper also. With this objective in mind National Mission for

Manuscripts decided to organize some workshops on the conservation of such manuscripts at different venues for the benefit of those who are responsible for handling such manuscripts. Since it was not possible for all those who are involved in the maintenance of such collections to attend these workshops, it was considered useful to publish the write-ups on the conservation of such manuscripts in the form of a book for future reference for all such persons.

This volume contains articles on the conservation of manuscripts on palm leaves, parchment, ivory, cloth, *sanchipat* and metals. The inputs for the volume were provided by a number of conservators. B.V. Kharbade discussed the scientific study of *kaditas* (manuscripts on cloth) and their conservation, while V. Jeyaraj discussed the storage and general guidelines for handling and care of manuscripts on different support materials. Achal Pandya, and D.D.N.Singh dealt with different aspects of technique of fabrication and conservation of metal manuscripts. Samiran Boruah discussed the historical and technical aspects of miniature paintings in the manuscripts of Assam, while D.G.Suryawanshi gave an experimental account on the conservation of birch bark manuscripts. The volume also contains articles on the technique of making, deterioration and conservation methods for manuscripts on parchment, palm leaf and ivory. The articles deal with the anatomy of the manuscripts in different media, but more particularly with the conservation aspect.

The papers in the volume contain a wealth of information on various aspects of the materials of manuscripts other than paper, and strategies for their conservation and maintenance.

First paper in the volume entitled 'Conservation of Manuscripts on Palm Leaves' discusses the types of palm leaves, their preparation and the mechanism of their deterioration. This is followed by the description of conservation procedures, which included the methods of cleaning, regaining of flexibility, re-inking, reinforcement and reintegration of manuscript folios of palm leaves.

The paper entitled 'Metals, Materials and their Preservation' deals with the history of discovery and scientific basis of the properties of metals and their alloys. This also discusses the methods of removal of corrosion and how to control recurrence of corrosion, with specific reference to copper.

The paper 'Deterioration and Conservation of copper Artifacts' discusses in detail the mechanism of formation of corrosion on artifacts of copper and its alloys depending upon the composition of the artifacts and the environment these are exposed to. Though it does not specifically involve manuscripts, but the theory is quite relevant to manuscripts made out of copper and its alloys. The paper also deals with the chemical interaction for removal of corrosion from copper and its alloys.

Metals have sometimes been used as support material for manuscripts because of some of their useful properties. The paper entitled 'Conservation of Manuscripts on Metals with Special Reference to Copper' discusses the properties of metals and history of their extraction. This is followed by the discussion on formation of various types of corrosion on manuscripts made out of copper and its alloys under different conditions, and finally the conservation procedures for removal, preservation, sealing or inhibiting the recurrence of their corrosion.

The paper 'Miniature Paintings of the Assamese Manuscripts' discusses in detail the historical and technical aspect of the miniature paintings incorporated in the manuscripts of Assam. These paintings illustrate the events described in the text and so the knowledge of text of manuscripts is almost essential to appreciate these paintings.

Sanchipat is the support material for manuscripts used in North-eastern states of the country, such as Assam, Tripura and Meghalaya. It is made out the bark of agar wood tree. The paper 'Conservation of *Sanchipat* Manuscripts' discusses the method of making of *sanchipat* manuscripts, their deterioration and conservation methods. It discusses preventive conservation as well as curative conservation procedures such as cleaning , straightening and reinforcement.

Kadita is a long piece of cloth applied with a thick paste of ground tamarind seeds and charcoal powder, which looks like a thick black paper, used as a support material for manuscripts in different parts of Karnataka. The paper 'Preliminary Report on the Conservation of *Kaditas* (black manuscripts)' deals with the survey, scientific examination, deterioration and conservation of some *Kaditas* in Regional Conservation Laboratory, Mysore.

Ivory is another material which has sometimes been used as support material for manuscripts. Not only the tusk of elephant, the tusks and teeth from walrus, hippopotamus, boar, and whales are also commonly referred to as ivory. The paper 'Conservation of Manuscripts on Ivory' discusses the processing of ivory to make it suitable as writing material, its deterioration and conservation, which includes its cleaning, straightening and reinforcement.

Birch bark is a support material obtained from the bark of the Paper Birch tree (*Betula papyrifera*), which grows at high altitude. In India this has been used in Kashmir. The paper 'Studies on Methods of Lamination of Birch Bark Manuscripts', discusses the results of experimental study on different methods of lamination of birch bark manuscripts.

Throughout the entire Middle Ages, parchment, alongside papyrus, was the predominant writing material in Europe, the Near and Middle East. It is obtained from the skin of animals, such as sheep and goats. This has been found to be very durable as compared to paper and so often been used for documents required to be permanent. The article 'Conservation of Manuscripts on Parchment' discusses the manufacture, deterioration and conservation methods of parchment manuscripts.

Storage and handling is one of the most important aspects of preventive conservation of manuscripts. Creating of proper storage conditions and proper handling take care of the whole collection without much of the efforts. The paper 'Storage of Manuscripts and Conservation Guidelines' discusses various storage devices and guidelines for handling the manuscripts on different support materials.

Responsibility of the statements made in the articles published in the volume however rests solely with the authors. The views expressed by any individual are not necessarily those of Editor or of NMM.

The volume is meant for custodians of manuscripts, beginners in manuscript conservation and those conservators who want to understand the scientific aspect of deterioration and subsequent conservation of materials used as support materials for manuscripts. It is hoped that it would be able to fulfill its function, and thus contributing towards the preservation of this form of National Heritage.

K.K. GUPTA

January 26th 2010
New Delhi

1

Conservation of Manuscripts on Palm Leaves

K.K. Gupta

Many materials, such as clay, leaves, bark, stone, ivory, metals, wood and parchment have been used to write on in the past. Among them palm leaf was one of the most popular writing supports in India before the advent of paper. We come across a large number of palm leaf manuscripts in the collection of museums, and in other manuscript repositories.

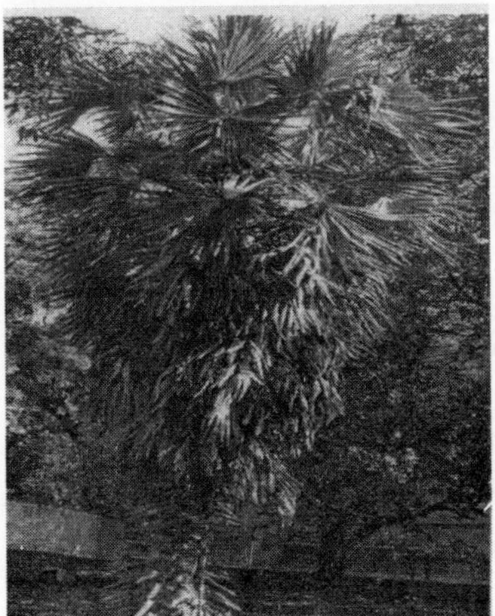

Palmyra Palm

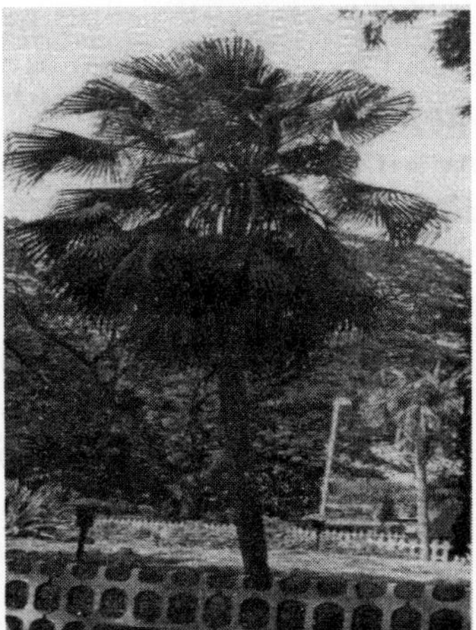

Talipot Palm

Preparation of Palm Leaf Manuscripts

Leaves from many types of palm trees have been used for writing purposes. Most common among them being *Khartala* or *Tala* obtained from Palmyra Palm *(Borassus flabelliformis)* and *Sritala* from Talipot Palm (*Corypha umbraculifera*). *Tala* leaf is thick and coarse and breaks easily, while *Sritala* is relatively thin, long, smooth and flexible and is more resistant to decay. Various methods were adopted in order to prepare these leaves suitable for writing on them and the methods of preparation used to vary from one region to another.

In Indian subcontinent, the palm leaves are boiled in water, dried and then buried in silts for a long period of time. They are then cleaned and dried in sun for some time; turmeric paste is then applied over the leaves. In some cases the leaves are boiled in lime water to make them thin and soft. In South India, gingelli oil is employed to make the surface smooth for writing.

When palm leaves became dry, citronella oil, lemon grass oil, olive oil, etc. were applied on them to increase their flexibility. Since palm leaves could not be bound, these are generally placed between two wooden boards and are tied with strings passing through two holes drilled in these boards.

Tal-patra manuscripts are usually found in the form of bundles of fifty to hundred, strung together with a cord and pressed between two wooden boards. Some collections also have meter-long uncut leaves, with mid-ribs intact, rolled like a carpet. *Tala* leaves do not absorb writing ink and so the text has to be incised into the surface of the leaf with a pointed metal stylus and then lamp black or pigment powder is rubbed into the letters. Writing is sometimes made visible by rubbing some fresh green leaves into it for depositing their juice in groove thereby creating a contrast. *Sritala,* on the other hand, is absorbent like paper and hence texts can be written on its surface with pen and ink.

Deterioration

Palm leaves are organic in nature and thus are susceptible

to decay like any other organic material. The chief constituent of palm leaves is cellulose while other constituents are gums, resins, pigments and essential oils. The main factors responsible for the deterioration of palm leaves are temperature, humidity, light, pollution, insect attack, wrong handling and storage.

In consequence of the combined action of all these deteriorating factors, the palm leaves become yellow and brittle resulting in their breaking into pieces. Other problems encountered in case of palm leaves are dust and dirt accumulation, loss of ink and sticking of the folios.

Natural oil present in the leaves acts as preservative and lubricant and so provides them the flexibility. But after a certain period the oil partially evaporates and partially polymerizes resulting in loss of flexibility of the leaves. Insect attack on the palm leaves, not only eats away their material, but also causes the leaves sticking together due to their excreta. This type of problem is more commonly found in *Tala* leaves. Frequent and improper opening and binding of the manuscripts also leads to the widening of holes meant for cord used for binding of the manuscript folios, and ultimately to the breakage of the folios.

Conservation

Conservation of palm leaves can be classified into preventive and curative conservation.

Preventive Conservation is the control of factors of deterioration responsible for the decay of manuscripts. Preventive conservation is non-interactive and takes care of the whole collection simultaneously. For the vast collection of manuscripts all over the country, preventive conservation seems to be the more practical solution.

Keeping in mind that most chemical and biological reactions can be slowed down by lowering ambient temperature, the recommended optimum temperature for a display or storage area of manuscripts is between 20° and

25°C. Also since the fluctuations in temperature causes more deterioration to palm leaf folios, sharp fluctuations in the temperature should not be allowed even within these limits. Relative humidity (RH) in the area also should neither be too high nor too low as both these conditions may result in dimensional strain on palm leaves, leading to their deterioration. The recommended RH for manuscripts is between 45 and 55 percent, again without sharp fluctuations even within these limits. These limits of temperature and RH, however, can be shifted a bit, depending on the average values of the outer atmosphere. The intention behind this is to reduce the difference between inner and outer temperature as well as their R.H., and thereby to reduce the probability of their sharp changes and thus making their maintenance easier.

The light even though is a potent factor of deterioration, is essential for reading a manuscript; and so it is considered to be a necessary evil. The recommended upper limit of intensity of light and its ultraviolet proportion are 50 Lux and 50 microwatt per Lumen respectively, in case of palm leaf manuscripts. Also, since the deteriorating effect of light is cumulative, apart from its intensity, the time of exposure of the manuscript to light should be minimized. The ultra videt(UV) content of the light should also be minimum. This can be done by a judicious selection of a light source and use of UV filters. Incandescent bulbs, for example, have low UV content but since they generate heat waves causing an adverse effect on palm leaves, temperature needs to be controlled if these are used. UV filters should be used over the light sources if their light is not free from UV.

Atmospheric pollution, especially due to increasing industrialization, has also been playing a major role in the degradation of palm leaves. The effect of pollution can be controlled to some extent by taking some measures so that pollution cannot reach manuscript repositories. In order to do that, one needs to develop green belts in the vicinity of the repositories or to make arrangements for treating incoming air free from all pollutants. Green belt, however, may increase the humidity in the area.

Biological factors like insects and fungi also play a significant role in the decay of palm leaf manuscripts. It is, therefore, important to eradicate these from storage or display areas of the manuscripts. This can be done by keeping the collection and the related areas neat and clean, and by using insect-repellant or insecticides in order to nip the problem in the bud. Fumigation with para di chloro benzene has been found to be useful as a repellant as well as insecticide. Its fumes being heavier than air, it is kept in the uppermost shelf of the fumigation chamber with a concentration of 1.5 kg per cubic meter. A mixture of carbon disulphide and carbon tetra chloride (1:3) has also been found effective for eradicating the insects. Fumigation with these chemicals kills living larvae and adults, but the eggs are not affected. So in order to eradicate the insects in all the stages of their growth, the fumigation with these may be repeated after three weeks.

Since the chemicals used as repellants and insecticides are likely to be toxic to human beings also, some non-chemical methods such as deep freezing, heating and creating an oxygen-free atmosphere are also being used to eradicate the insects from the collections.

Apart from these measures mentioned above it is very important to use right methods for handling the manuscripts to save the manuscripts from further decay. Following precautions may be taken while handling:

- Avoid stacking, wherever possible.
- Do not unnecessarily touch the leaves with bare hands.
- Wear white cotton gloves while handling these or clean and dry the hands before handling.
- Protect the manuscripts from dust and dirt.
- While storing these, wrap them in acidfree tissue paper

or unbleached de-starched cotton cloth.

- Clean them with a soft dry brush.
- If air-conditioning is used, it should be round the clock and with continuous monitoring of temperature and RH.
- Arrange proper ventilation to avoid any stagnation of air.
- Clean the storage/display area regularly.
- Do not keep the manuscripts in contact with metals.
- Shelving to keep the objects off the floor.
- Inspect and clean the manuscripts regularly

Curative Conservation

Curative conservation of palm leaf manuscripts can be classified into:

- Cleaning
- Regaining the flexibility
- Re-inking
- Re-inforcement
- Re-integration

Cleaning

Palm leaf presents a peculiar problem as regards its cleaning, because of the roughness of its surface. Normal cleaning with a dry cotton swab would not remove the dust as it remained trapped in crevices of the rough surface. The fibres of cotton, on the contrary, get trapped there. Loose dust and dirt is, therefore, better removed by the use of soft dry brush. Hard encrustations can also be removed mechanically by the use of sharp scalpel or other suitable tools. Care should however be taken, that it may not result in further physical damage.

If simple mechanical methods fail to remove the incrustations or are too risky, these can be removed after softening with the help of a small amount of water or some organic solvent, as the case may be. Surface of the written texts may be cleaned by the use of organic solvents as prolonged contact with water may result in the bleeding of ink. Incised text, however, is somewhat resistant to water and so mixture of water and alcohol can be used. Cotton wrapped in muslin cloth moistened with a mixture of water and alcohol can be employed for general cleaning of *Tāla* palm leaves. Cleaning strokes should always follow the line of grains to avoid any damage across the grains.

Regaining of flexibility

A dry climate or the evaporation of volatile components of age-old palm leaves results in decrease in their flexibility, and make them brittle and fragile. Citronella, camphor or lemon oil have often been used for imparting flexibility to brittle palm leaves. Since these oils attract dust resulting in soiling of the leaves, these need to be cleaned repeatedly. Mixture of alcohol and glycerin has also been used for cleaning and imparting flexibility simultaneously to palm leaves.

As a result of storage of the manuscripts in humid conditions and because of the weight of overlying manuscripts, the palm leaves sometimes stick together, and become a solid mass. The leaves in such cases may be separated by exposing the mass to humidity in a humidity chamber, or to steam. When they become sufficiently moist, each leaf is separated carefully by introducing a fine spatula between them. Alcohol bath can also be used for separating the stuck-up palm leaf folios.

Re-inking

In case of *Śritāla* palm leaf manuscripts, the writing is on the surface and the ink used has a binding medium. Once lost, the ink cannot be regained in such cases. So if the ink has the tendency of flaking or powdering because of the degradation of binding medium of the ink, it can be consolidated by the application of 1% solution of paraloid

B72 in toluene or acetone, which may be repeated if the ink is still powdery on flaking.

Ink in case of *Tāla* palm leaf manuscripts, does not contain any binding medium and is only held mechanically in the groves created by stylus. The loss of ink in this case is mainly because of the abrasion due to repeated handling. In some cases the application of ink was missed out even at the time of creating the manuscripts. Re-inking in *Tāla* palm leaf manuscripts is done to make them legible by the application of suspension of powdered carbon in comphor oil all over the leaf, and then removing the excess after a day.

Re-inforcement

Re-inforcement refers to repair and strengthening of the damaged and weakened folios.Tear in the palm leaves, when there is no loss, can be repaired by the use of PVA emulsion at the torn edges. If the palm leaf is thin, the joint may not attain enough strength as the area of adhesion is too less. In such cases, to increase the area of adhesion, fine tissue paper of good quality protruding about 0.2 cm. beyond the tear on both sides, is used. The losses in the leaves and holes can be repaired with putty made of tissue paper pulp/powder of dry palm leaves and a suitable amount of adhesive such as Methyl Cellulose or PVA emulsion.

In case of palm leaves which are are very weak and fragile all over and cannot be provided reasonable strength by local repairs, these are lined with tissue paper or chiffon, with starch paste, CMC or methyl cellulose as adhesive. The lining material. i. e. tissue paper or chiffon chosen should be sufficiently transparent so that it can provide re-inforcement and yet the writing remains suficiently visible. In extreme cases of deterioration, the palm leaf manuscripts, are laminated, as a last resort.

Re-integration

There is often a tendency of further aggravation of damage

if there are losses in the leaves. The lost areas are, therefore, restored to avoid their further damage. This can be done by inserting the pieces of palm leaves of similar thickness, strength and texture as of the original. The pieces are cut to the size and shape of the loss with similar fibre directions, and fixed in position by PVA emulsion as adhesive. Fine gaps can be filled with a putty made from powder of dry palm leaves with PVA emulsion as adhesive. Prepared wood veneer, having paper as interleaf, has also been used for restoration of the losses. Care should, however, be taken that the restored area has a strength comparable with the original, and is not too strong.

Palm leaf has been one of the very imporatant materials used in India for the purpose of writing. As in all the cases of antiquities, preventive care of the palm leaf manuscripts should be the first priority to protect these from any deterioration. Methods and materials for the curative conservation of palm leaf manuscripts need to be carefully chosen, so as to have minimum side and after effects.

2

Metals, Materials and their Preservation

D.D.N. Singh

METALS ARE known to human being for more than six millennia. It is believed that the first metal known to human being was gold, which was discovered as it exists in a metallic form in the nature. This was followed by the discovery of copper, silver, etc. All these metals are nobler (immune to normal corrosive conditions) and they existed abundantly at many places. Ancient people living near to these places got interested in these metals due to their lustrous and colourful appearances. They used them for making ornaments and sharp weapons as well. Since the metals were found to be malleable in nature, people gradually developed novel technology of hammering to make them as foil. The understanding of processes of metals and their mechanical, magnetic and electronic properties also followed with their discoveries. This was catalyzed by the discovery of modern equipments that helped to understand the insight of metals.

Now it is possible to explain different behaviours of metals and alloys by considering their atomic structures and arrangement of crystal structures, inter-metallic bonding, crystal defects, etc. Discovery of electron microscopy which helped to see the tiny particles by magnifying them several hundreds thousands times, catalyzed the understanding of science of metals and alloys.

It is inherent in the nature of human beings to amalgamate many things together and observe the outcome of these amalgamations. This tendency led to the development of alloys comprising of different metals from different compositions. Mixing of these metals resulted in phenomenal improvement in the properties of alloys.

Importance of Metals in Archaeology

On 26th November 1950, Pt. Jawahar Lal Nehru, our first prime minister and the great visionary, while inaugurating the National Metallurgical Laboratory at Jamshedpur, expressed his feelings as follows:

"To ignore the past, throw it away, means to throw away the whole foundation on which we have grown." Since most of the invaluable knowledge that our ancestors had, are still hidden in artefacts which are in the form of metals and alloys, their understanding to archaeologists are of great importance. The studies of archaeology provides invaluable information not only about art and culture of the ancient people but also what may lead us to newer and frontier areas of research in different fields. Studies of ancient metallic artefacts occupy special position particularly for nobler metals which withstand climatic effects on their properties. Before we go more into details about wealth of knowledge that many of our ancient artifacts have preserved in them, it will be prudent to provide brief background about the metals, metallurgy and their properties.

Historical Background about the Metals

Metals are blessed with many unparallelled properties such as high thermal and electrical conductivity, opaque but lustrous, heavy and deformable and normally good reflector of light. Owing to these properties ancient people got interested in them. Gold, because of its lusture and good colour, was the first to be discovered in about 5000 BC.

Thereafter, other metals were discovered. A plot showing the metals discovered before the christian era is shown in Fig. 1.

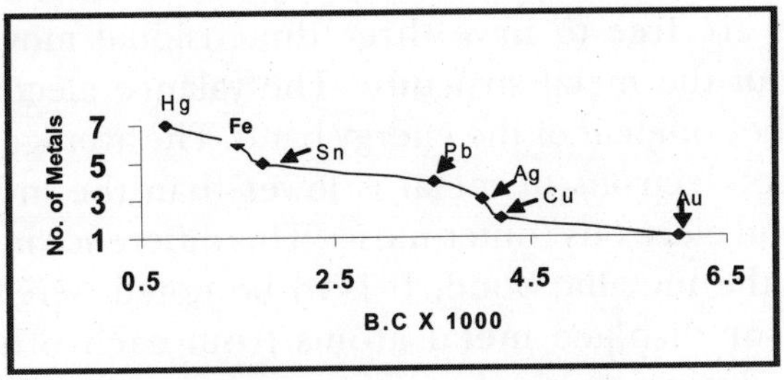

Fig. 1 Discovery of Metals BC

•Delocalized electrons: Outermost bonding electrons free to have three dimensional move through metal structure

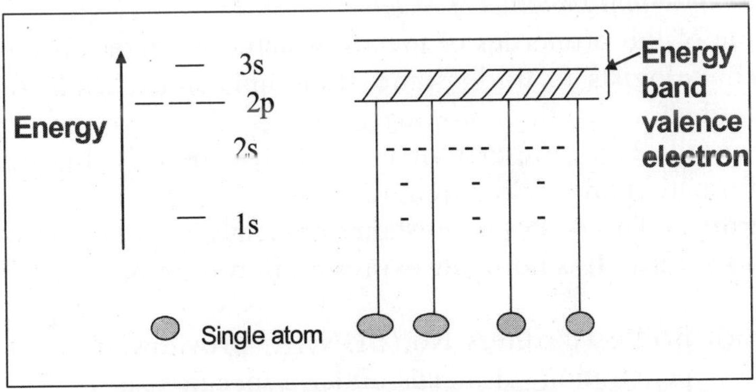

Sodium–Na–Atomic Number 11
Electronic arrangement $1s^2$, $2s^2$, $2p^6$, $3s^1$

Fig. 2 Electronic structure of metals and bonding in their atoms

Bonding in Atoms of Metals

In order to explain the unique properties of metals such as high melting point, strength, etc. it is important to understand the bonding between atoms of metals. This can be understood by considering the electronic arrangement of sodium atom as shown in Fig. 2.

It is seen from the figure that the outer-most bonding electrons are free to have three dimensional movements throughout the metal structure. The valance electrons fill only the bottom half of the energy band. The average energy of valance electrons of metal is lower than the individual atoms bond electrons (outer-most). This difference in energy provides the metallic bond. It is to be noted here that to separate or displace metal atoms from each other, for example, during melting, working, etc., one has to supply outer energy. More the energy difference between valance electrons and individual atoms bond electrons exists, the higher will be their melting point and it is difficult to deform them.

Some Important Properties of Metals

Some of the properties of metals, which are important for archaeologists to understand their behaviour, shall be described under the following headings:

Strength: This property of metal helps to resist plastic deformation and yields strength to it;

Hardness: This relates to resistance of metals for penetration of its surface. It is normally expressed in two units;

(a) Bridle Hardness No.(BHN): It provides area of penetration of metals under a specific load;
(b) Rockwell Hardness: This provides depth of penetration of metal surface under a specific load;

Plastic Deformation and Recrystallization

The plastically deformed crystals bear more energy than non-deformed one. To bring them in normal condition, higher temperature treatments are provided in metals to recrystallize strained crystals. Annealing reduces their hardness and minimum temperature required to reduce hardness after plastic deformation is known as the annealing temperature.

Effect of Alloying on Properties of Metals

A solid solution is formed when solvent and solute of alloying metals are very close in their atomic sizes and comparable in electronic structure. Some of the solid solution compositions related to copper is shown in Table 1. It is seen from the table that copper and zinc are very close in their atomic radii as well as in valence electrons and therefore form a solid solution. Similarly for alloying of copper and nickel to form monel metal, they can be mixed in any ratio as their atomic radii are very close to each other. In general, it is observed that when difference in atomic radii is less than 15%, a solid solution is formed.

Table 1: Effect of atomic radii and electronic structure on alloying properties of metals
Solid Soultions

Solvent & solute —> similar sizes
—> Comparable electronic structure

Brass:	Copper	Zinc	Solid Solution Composition
Radii	1.278	1.39	60:40
Subvalent electrons	28		
Monel	Copper	Ni	
	1.278	1.246	Any ratio
Broze	Copper	Tin	90:10
Al-Bronze	Copper	Al	
	1.278	1.431	80:20
Sterling Silver	Copper	Ag	75 : 92.5
Difference in Atomic radil <15%			

Copper and Copper based Alloys, their Deterioration and Preservation

The copper and copper based alloys are relatively noble metals that frequently survive adverse conditions, including long submersions in salt water. Copper based alloys removed from sea water are covered with cuprous chloride (CuCl), cupric chloride ($CuCl_2$) and cuprous oxide (Cu_2O). The artefacts removed from soil are often covered with aesthetically pleasing green- and blue-coloured cupric carbonates–malachite [$Cu_2(OH)_2CO_3$] and azurite [$Cu_3(OH)_2(CO_3)_2$], in addition to these corrosion products. In a marine environment, the two most commonly encountered copper corrosion products are cuprous chloride and cuprous sulfide. The corrosion products formed on copper alloys, however, vary depending upon the types of environments surrounding the artefacts.

In case of the artefacts submerged in deep sea where comparatively anaerobic conditions persists, the copper-based articles develop cuprous chloride on their surface:

$Cu = Cu^+ + e^-$

$NaCl = Na^+ + Cl^-$ (From sea water)

$Cu^+ + Cl^- = CuCl$ (Cuprous Chloride)

Cuprous chlorides are very unstable mineral compounds, and the freshly recovered copper objects covered with cuprous chlorides undergo transformations in the presence of atmosphere (having moisture and oxygen) to form cupric chloride and hydrochloric acid :

$$4CuCl + 4H_2O + O_2 = CuCl_2\ 3Cu(OH)_2 + 2HCl$$

The hydrochloric acid released in the above reaction, in turn, attacks the virgin metal to form more cuprous chloride:

$$2Cu + 2HCl = 2CuCl + H_2$$

In this way, a vicious cycle develops and the reactions continue until whole metal gets converted into cupric chloride. This chemical corrosion process is commonly referred to as 'bronze disease.' Any conservation of chloride-contaminated cuprous objects requires that the chemical action of the chlorides be inhibited either by removing or converting them to harmless cuprous oxide.

In many instances the copper objects in sea water also get converted to cuprous and cupric sulfide (Cu_2S and CuS) by the action of sulphate-reducing bacteria. In anaerobic environments, the copper sulfide products are usually in the lowest oxidation state. In this case also, like cuprous chloride, the cuprous sulphide film present on artefacts, after recovery and exposure to oxygen, undergoes the subsequent transformation to a higher oxidation state, i.e. cupric sulfide. The reaction proceeds on the identical lines as described above for chlorides. The stable copper sulfide layer, however, is not as deleterious as copper chlorides. They only discolour the artefacts and make their look unaesthetic.

Methods for Controlling the Corrosion of Copper and Copper based Alloys

As described above, copper and copper based alloys are ordinarily immune in normal neutral environments. However, they are attacked if the environment contains complexing agents such as chloride, fluoride, sulphides, organic acids, amines etc. This is the reason that most of the artefacts found remain covered with different types of copper compounds. Before going for their preservation, it is important that they are made free from the harmful corrosion products. Different techniques are employed for their cleaning . The following methods are commonly employed:

1. Electrolytic Cleaning: In this method of cleaning, the artefact is cleaned in a suitable electrolyte by making

its whole surface as cathode. In this method of cleaning, the corrosion products on the surface are reduced either in metallic form or get converted into a soluble salt. Thus no attacks on the surface of the metals take place and original shape of the artefact remains intact. Either 2 percent sodium hydroxide or 5 percent sodium carbonate can be used as electrolyte. In some cases , 5 percent formic acid is also used as the electrolyte. 316 grade stainless steel or platinized titanium is used as the anode.

2. Electroless Reductive Dissolution: In this method some formulated special solutions are used for cleaning of copper and copper based artefacts. These solutions react only with the corrosion products and transform them to metal or soluble complex salts . This method is very effective and easy to apply.

In both these methods all the compounds of copper are removed including those which are protective in nature. These methods are, therefore, rarely used in case of antiquities.

Preservation: The various common methods used in corrosion protection of metals and alloys are also employed to preserve copper and copper based artefacts. They can be classified as follows:

(a) Development of protective patina on the surface
(b) Providing of poly organic coats
(c) Application of moisture resistant transparent coatings
(d) Modified polyvinyl + alkyd resin coatings

(a) Development of Protective Patina: Copper and copper based alloys form oxides that are highly protective in nature, especially if developed under controlled conditions. These patina provide excellent aesthetic look and protect the underneath metal surface very effectively. They become more effective in protecting the metal when they are treated by specially formulated solutions. These formulations help to form the well structured and pore- free oxides on the surface.

(b) Poly-organic Coats: These types of coatings, although form very protective layer and remain stable in mild environments, are prone to deterioration under aggressive conditions. Self assembled molecules (SAM) of triazole and its derivatives form very stable film on copper surface. In this method of treatment, the benzo triazole or its derivative dissolved in a suitable organic solvent are applied on the copper based artefacts. They form very protective film and develop the resistance of the order of mega Ohm. They can be used as the under coat followed by the application of a thin transparent coating.

(c) Moisture Resistant Coatings: Different types of waxes are used to protect copper based artefacts. Their adhesion to the surface, especially on contaminated surface, however is normally very poor. This results in faster deterioration in humid and hot environments.

(d) Modified Polyvinyl Coating: There are some materials available in the market which are based on modified polyvinyl polymers. These polymers develop very effective bonding even with the surface containing oxide. These types of coatings can be tried on copper and copper based artefacts without removing natural patina already formed on their surface.

3

Deterioration and Conservation of Copper Artifacts

Achal Pandya

COPPER metal, on account of its low ionization potential looses some electrons and changes into positive ions Cu^+ and $Cu.^{2+}$ The electrons released in this manner are not localized. They are mobile and thus keep the Cu^+ ions hold together. As the copper comes in contact with air (O_2^-), oxidation of metal occurs and the first primary contact layer is formed i.e. of cuprite $Cu_2 O$. But this cuprite layer conducts electronically owing to the process of ionic defects in cuprite and leads to the further deterioration. This type of corrosion is known as "dry corrosion."

As corrosion continues, the dissolved Cu^+ ions migrate to the surface of cuprite and subjected to the reaction with environment around it. This may lead to the formation of layer of basic carbonates and basic chlorides.

Possible reactions that take place during copper corrosion are

In presence of oxygen

In dry conditions—

$$Cu^+ + O_{2-} \rightarrow Cu_2 O$$

This reaction takes place when copper artifacts are kept in clean and dry environment.

In presence of water and oxygen, the reduction reaction is

$$\frac{1}{2} O_2 + H_2 O + 2e^- \rightarrow OH^-$$

Followed by oxidation of Cu^{2+}

$$Cu^+ \xrightarrow{[O]} Cu^{++}$$

Final reaction is

$$Cu^{++} + 2OH^- \rightarrow Cu(OH)_2 \text{ (In wet conditions)}$$

The above reactions take place when the object is in contact of humid environments.
In the presence of CO_2

A. *In the presence of CO_2:*

$$Cu(OH)_2 + CO_2 \rightarrow CuCO_3Cu(OH)_2 \text{ (Malachite)}$$

$$Cu(OH) + CO_2 \rightarrow 2CuCO_3Cu(OH)_2 \text{ (Azurite)}$$

The corrosion layers of basic carbonates formed on copper artifacts are uniform and provide protection to the object from further corrosion and enhance the aesthetic appearance of the artifact. Copper artifact may get covered with these copper (II) carbonate hydroxides when copper objects are found from humid, closed places, buried places where the ixidation of organic compuunds may generate high level of carbon doixide.

In Industrial environment

Out door exposure of copper based artifacts in the industrial environment are particularly subjected to the corrosion in the presence of $H_2 S$ and SO_2 .[1]

$$SO_2 + H_2O \rightarrow H_2\ SO_3 \xrightarrow{[O]} H_2\ SO_4$$
$$Cu^{++} + H_2\ SO_4 \longrightarrow'\ Cu\ SO_4$$
$$Cu\ (OH)_2 + Cu\ SO_4 \rightarrow 2Cu\ SO_4\ 3Cu\ (OH)_2$$
[Brochanlite vitreous green]

The other example of corrosion in outdoor environments such as exposed to rain of low pH (acid rain) is the formation of antlerite.[2]

$$Cu_2O \xrightarrow{[O]} CuO + H_2SO_4 + H_2O \rightarrow CuSO_4\ 2Cu\ (OH)_2$$
(Anterlite Vitreous green)

In the presence of chlorides

In the chloride atmosphere, copper corrosion can be very serious and may result, what is known as bronze disease. Bronze disease is a progessive deterioration of ancient copper alloys caused by the existence of cuprous chloride (nantokite) in close proximity to whatever metallic surface may remain.[3] Cuprous chloride may lie dormant until reaction with moisture and oxygen causes this unstable compound to expand in volume on conversion to one of the copper trihydroxychlorides. This creates physical stress within the object affected, resulting in cracking or fragmentation. Symptoms on coppoer alloy with bronze disease are:

1. If occurs in isolated spots
2. Presence of pale green powder in isolated spots
3. It may result in the formation of warts, having cuprous chloride and copper trihydroxychlorides.

In moist conditions, in objects suffering from bronze disease, there is a production of HCl during the formation of $Cu_2Cl(OH)_3$ (copper trihydroxychlorides) which leads to the further deterioration of copper.[3-5]

If only a small amount of nantokite is present, it is possible that the corrosion will stop once the chloride ions have been incorporated into solid copper (II) chloride hydroxide. However, if there is a thick layer of nantokite on archaeological copper alloys, it may be enough to cause corrosion of all the remaining metal and total distruction of the object.[5]

The chlorides in copper artifacts can come from the burial environment or when these are excavated from marine environment. The objects having chloride attack, when found from these environments, are termed as surffering from bronze disease. Objects kept near the sea coast may also get exposure to chlorides. For example author while cleaning copper alloy artifacts at Pondicherry Museum, which is situated very close to the sea shore, noticed that the objects of copper and its alloys were suffering from bronze disease. The salt laden winds in these regions which may lead to the formation of cuprous chloride in presence of moisture, and then to the formation of cuprous chloride hydroxides. Selwyn calls such type of attack as non traditional bronze disease.[5]

Corrosion Caused by Sodium Contamination

Copper artifacts lying underground may react with salts containing sodium ions resulting in the formation of unusual corrosion product known as chalconatronite $Na_2Cu(CO_3)_2 3H_2O$. This product may also be formed due to the previous conservation treatment given to copper objects using products like sodium hydroxide, sodium sesquicarbonate, alkaline glycerol, alkaline rochelle's salt, sodium hexameta phosphate, sodium tri poly phosphate etc[5-6]

The formation of chalconatronite is linked to the formation of $[Cu(CO_3)_2]^{2+}$ ion. This may react with the additional sodium ion leading to the formation of bluish corrosion product known as cahalconatronite. Blue coloured corrosion product may also be formed due to the release organic fumes of acetic acids form wood, paint or any other source in the show cases. The product is blue or turquoise in colour and is generally described as CuNa $(CH_3\ CO_2)$ (CO_3)[5,7]

Corrosion in Different types of Copper Alloys

(1) *In Brasses (Copper and Zinc)*

As expected from the electrochemical series, zinc being the anodic component will corrode preferentially to copper, Brasses having more than 15% of zinc are also prone to destabilization process known as dezincification. Desincification is more common in Cl^- rich environments and when brasses are exposed to low pH solutions.[8,9]

(2) *In High Tin Bronzes*

Tin being upper in the electrochemical series is anodic to copper. The corrosion of tin normally results in the accumulation of the insoluble tin oxides (SnO_2). This impedes the further anodic process of destannification, or tin dissolution. Tin oxide results in the formation of white or grey patina called water patina and it is very inert in nature.[8]

(3) *In Leaded Bronzes*

Since lead in insoluble in copper at room temperature, it is usually present in the form of discrete globules as a separate phase from the copper alloy. This segregation can result in severe corrosion of lead phase. The globules are surrounded by a largely cathodes copper region; this can cause the lead to become oxidized to the basic carbonates or oxides. Organic acids, such as those found in unsuitable storage conditions, may interact preferentially with these globules, producing a whitish surface haze to the copper based artifacts or more severe corrosion excrescence. Such excrescences were noted by Dr. Tej Singh et al while working on leaded bronzes in RCL, Mysore. In some cases, a combination of copper corrosion and lead corrosion may result in next copper lead materialization on the surface.[8, 10]

(4) *In Arsenical and Antimonial Alloys of Copper*
Arsenical and Antimonial alloys of copper may also undergo the type of deterioration that takes place in leaded bronzes, although here the elements forms solid solutions of various types. However, segregation is still possible, especially due to casting, which may result in dendrites segregation and coring of the intradendritic regions.[8]

Treatment of artifacts made up of copper and its alloys
The treatment of copper and its alloys is varied and depends upon the type of copper alloy and problem present. Detailed documentation and examination is a must before the commencement of any conservation treatment. As discussed above the corrosion on the copper and its alloys depends upon the type of alloy and the conditions from which it was obtained. It is also a well known fact that the most of the corrosion products of copper are harmless and stable and act as protective patina on the artifact. They may or may not be removed depending upon the objects requirements. In some cases they are thinned down to reveal the details of the object. This process is known as cleaning of the object. It can be done mechanically using microcope and fine tools like glass-fibre brushes, painting brushes, dental picks, a pin held in pin-vice, wooden tools or sticks by using some fine inert powder like chalk or ash. Sand blasting can also be used. The advantage of mechanical cleaning is that the treatment is controlled and there is nothing added to object to be washed out. Other treatment given to copper and its alloys for cleaning are electrolytic reduction. It employed electrolytic cell having an electrolyte and anode. Metal to be cleaned is made cathode. Electrolytic reduction of metal

is capable of removing all types of corrosion products present on copper. However if used with skill and care, electrolytic reduction can give good results. A new application of electrolysis for the dechlorination of copper alloys has also been developed. Electrolytic treatment with weak polarization in sodium sesquicarbonate permits the extraction of the chlorides and the preservation of stable alteration products.[11]

For cleaning of copper alloys they are immersed in 5% solution of sodium sesquicarbonate, Na HCO_3Na_2 CO_3. This treatment is successful in removing the chlorides from the surface but in artifacts, where $Cl^-$is seated inside the metal, this treatment has its limitations.[12] The treatment is very long and tedious, and requires dipping of artifacts in the solution, sometimes longer than a year. In addotion, the treatment of objects with this method may result in mineralogical changes in the patina, sometimes drastically altering the appearance of the copper alloys. Objects recovered from marine environment have also been treated with aqueous acetonitrile, CH_3CN, alkaline dithionite[13-14]

Other cleaning agents that have been used traditionally on copper alloys are alkaline glycerol, alkaline Rochelle salt, colague, citric acid, buffered citric acid, formic acid, ammonium hydroxide, ammonium bicitrate, sodium salt of EDTA, sodium hyroxide and dilute sulphuric acid. All these cleaning agents can cause itching of the metallic surface.[15] Sodium tripolyphosphate has also been used successfully for removal of calcareous deposits from the copper based artifacts.[16]

The treatments mentioned above are, mainly, the methods of cleaning and revealing the underneath layers of the metal. These methods generally do not cure the metals of further deterioration except in the treatment with sodium sesquicarbonate, where, there is the removal of chlorides from the copper artifacts. The limitation of this treatment has already been mentioned above. The problem caused in copper alloys due to presence of chlorides was diagnosed long back and conservators have been trying hard for their removal. Traditionally silver chloride and silver oxide have been used to stabilize the chloride present in copper artifacts. Later on chelating agents like benzotriazole (BTAH) was used to complex Cu ions and thus protect it from chloride attack. All these methods have their advantages and disadvantages. For, giving conservation treatment to copper artifacts suffering with bronze disease, there are three approaches

1. *Provide complexing treatment on their surface*
Two complexing agents have found place among the chemicals for this treatment. Benzotrizole (BTAH) is used extensively as complexing agent[17,18] Aminomercepto thiazole (AMT) was also tried.[19] AMT works well in complexing with copper ions; the only disadvantage is that it has some colour rendering on copper surface.[20] BTAH has problem in handling as it is potentially carcinogenic and needs great care while using it.[21]

2. *Immobilize chloride to make them innocuous*
In this approach traditionally silver oxide powder was used to seal the "bronze disease' pits locally. Sharma et al, however suggested that AgCl formed by this method does not provide protection as it conducts electronically and electrolytically. They came up with another method of sealing using zinc dust. During this treatment zinc hydroxide chlorides Zn $(OH)_2$ $ZnCl_2$ and 4Zn $(OH)_2$ $ZnCl_2$ are formed which act as a protective coating for the underlying metal. The unreacted zinc scavenges any other Cl^- present inside the metal or which can potentially enter from the environment.[22]

3. Provide colorless coating on the patina to provide complete retardation of reaction of the copper ions with chloine, moisture and air.

Traditionally different waxes, coatings like shellac have

been used to protect the underlying metal. Microcrystalline wax, polyvinyl acetate, paraloid B72 have also been and are still applied on the copper alloys as a protective coating. None of the above coatings has proved to provide the complete blocking of the deteriorating factors. Generation of certain products on aging of these protective coatings is also a matter of concern. Therefore, after the application of the protecting coating, the object should be monitored carefully and the coating should be removed once it starts to deteriorate, and reapplied.

Treatment of Leaded Bronzes

The pits formed in the leaded bronzes due to formation of lead carbonate are treated with neutral Benzotriazole. Neutral BTA forms polymeric, crystalline, thermally stable compound on the surface of metal. Pure analytically made calcium carbonate is used for neutralizing BTA.[9]

References

1. Stranberg, H. and Johansson, Journal of the Electrochemical Society (1988), 145, 1093-1100.
2. Scott, David A, Copper and Bronze in Art: Corrosion, Colorants, Conservation (2002), Getty Conservation Institute, Los Angeles, 145-67.
3. Ibid, 125-34.
4. Gilberg, M., Recent Advances in Conservation (1988), British Museum Publications Ltd, London, 59-70
5. Lyndsie, Selwyn, Metals and Corrosions: A Handbook for the Conservation Professional (2004), Canadian Conservation Institute, Ottawa, 51-71
6. Thickett, D. and Odlyha, M., Studies in Conservation (2000), 45, 63-67.
7. Bradley, S. and Thickett, D., 12th ICOM-CC Triennial Meeting Preprints (1999), 8-13.
8. Scott, David A., Copper and Bronze in Art: Corrosion, Colorants, Conservation (2002), Getty Conservation Institute, Los Angeles, 10-80.

9. Lucey, V.F., British Corrosion Journal (1972), 7, 36-41.
10. Sharma, V.C., Lal, Uma Shankar and Singh, Tej, Studies in Conservation (2003) 48, 203-209.
11. Pain, Silvia, Bertholon Regis, Lacoudre Noel (1991), 36, 33-43.
12. Oddy, W.A. and Hughes, M.J., Studies in Conservation (1970), 15, 183-189.
13. Macleod, Ian Donald, Studies in Conservation (1987), 32, 25-40.
14. Uminski M. and Guidelti V., Studies in Conservation (1995), 40, 274-278.
15. Scott, David A, Copper and Bronze in Art: Corrosion, Colorants, Conservation (2002), Getty Conservation Institute, Los Angeles, 366-367.
16. Sharma, V.C. and Kharbade, B.V. Stuides in Conservation (1994), 39, 39-44.
17. Organ, R.M., Museum Journal (1961), 61, 54-56.
18. Cotton, J. and Scholes, I., British Corrosion Journal (1967), 2, 1-5.
19. Ganorkar, M.C., Rao, V. Pandit, Gayathri, P. and Rao, T.A. Sreenivas, Studies in Conservation (1998), 32, 97-101.
20. Faltermeier, R.B. Studies in Conservation (1998), 32, 97-101.
21. Oddy, W.A. Studies in Conservation (1972), 17, 135.
22. Sharma, V.C., Lal, Uma Shankar and Nair, M. V., Studies in Conservation (1995) 40, 110-119,

4

Conservation of Manuscripts on Metals with Special Reference to Copper

K.K. Gupta

METALS HAVE also been used as a support for writings. The more common among these metals were copper, silver and gold. The metals have specific properties and are relatively more resistant to deterioration and hence these have sometimes been preferred for permanent records.

These properties which can be called metallic properties are as follows:

- Metals are solid at room temperature. Mercury is an exception to this property, and is liquid at room temperature.
- These have peculiar luster known as metallic lustre.
- Metals are malleable i.e. these can be beaten into thin sheets.
- These are ductile i.e. they can be drawn into thin wires.
- Most of the metals are hard (except sodium and potassium which are very soft.)
- Metals have high melting and boiling point (except sodium and potassium)
- Metals are generally good conductors of heat and electricity.

- Metals can form a homogeneous mixture in molten condition and this mixture is known as alloy.
- Most of the metals are sonorous, i.e. these produce sound.

Metals, though relatively more stable than organic materials, are quite reactive to their environmental conditions, with the exception of gold, platinum and silver, known as noble metals. It is due to this reason that very few metals occur in free form. Most of them occur in combined form as their compounds intermingled with sandy matter and other impurities. Various such compounds of metals, occurring in earth's crust, are called minerals.

It is generally agreed that the first metals came to be known were those which occur in the native state i.e. metallic state. So the earliest metal would in all probability be gold, found in sand or in the river bed before 4000 BC. Copper is another metal which is found in native state in many parts of the world.

The combination of various processes involved in the extraction of metals from their ores (minerals from which the metal can be extracted profitably) is known as metallurgy. The process to be used for the purpose varies from metal to metal.

Metals, because of their resistance to deterioration by environmental agencies as compared to other organic support material such as paper, have sometimes been preferred to be used as the support for manuscripts, particularly those required to be permanent. Gold and copper were the particular preferences for recording the inscriptions. The writing on these metals used to be created by casting, engraving or hammering.

Deterioration

Since these metals find their original natural mineralized form more stable, the moment these are extracted from their ores and fashioned into objects, they tend to revert back to their stable combined form. This reverse process which brings these metallic objects to the mineralized state is called the deterioration of these objects. The products so formed lack in metallic properties and cohesion and are in general, termed as corrosion. The corrosion is produced due to a series of chemical or electrochemical reactions, and the disintegration of the metal may be slow or accelerated depending upon the nature of the metal and the conditions to which it is exposed.

The continuous and smooth layer of corrosion on the metal surface is commonly known as patina. This gives an indication of the age of the object. Sometimes the patina is harmless to the object and acts as its protective layer. Such patina is termed as noble patina or protective patina and increases the aesthetic beauty of the object. Since the noble patina is protective for the object against further corrosion and increases the aesthetic beauty of the object, it should not be removed from the works of art unless it is obscuring some of its vital details. Even in such cases it is better to thin down the patina to expose the details rather than removing it completely. Some of the patinas are harmful to the object as they induce further corrosion and ultimately cause puncture in it. Such patinas are called malignant and should either be completely removed from the object or made passive. Sometimes metals are mixed with other metals or non-metals for the purpose of obtaining the material having some specific properties. These mixtures are known as alloys. However, the general behaviour of these alloys is close to the metal having the maximum proportion in these. In the alloys of copper such as brass, bronze, since the main component is copper, the corrosion is more or less like that of copper and the conservation treatment is also the same. Different coloured corrosions are found on copper and alloys of copper.

Blue: When copper alloys react with environment

containing dissolved carbon dioxide in the presence of oxygen. (usually during long burial) deep rooted blue coloured corrosion is formed on them. This blue colour is due to basic copper corbonate (Azurite). It is fragile and flakes off easily.

Green: Green coloured corrosion take place due to the formation of basic copper carbonate (Malachite), copper chloride (atacamite) or copper nitrate. While the carbonate and nitrate corrosions are protective in nature, chloride of copper leads to malignant and harmful corrosion commonly known as 'Bronze Disease.'

Black: Black corrosion is due to cupric oxide. Black carrosion may also be sometimes due to copper sulphide. These, however, are also protective in nature.

White: White patina on bronze is not very common and could be due to the formation of oxide of tin which is a component of some copper alloys.

Brown: Brown patina on copper alloys is due to cuprites (Cuprous oxide).

The green corrosion due to chloride is progressive in nature and so is considered malignant. This mechanism of the formation of perculiar, waxy, patchy, pale green powder is termed as 'Bronze Disease.' This proceeds due to transition of one form of chloride of coppr to other form under humid conditions, with the formation of hydrochloric acid till the metal gets completely mineralized.

Conservation

Conservation of metal objects involves three main operations:

1. Cleaning
2. Consolidation
3. Preservation

Cleaning

Cleaning of metal objects in a museum refers to the removal

of harmful incrustations to stop their further decay and to thin down the harmless ones to clear their details. In effect it means the removal of extraneous accumulations and harmful corrosion products of the metals and the thinning down of protective patina to expose the underlying details or inscriptions. Since this cleaning is an irreversible operation it should be carefully decided as to which incrustations are to be removed and to the extent of cleaning.

The noble patina, in addition to giving aesthetic beauty to the objects, resists their further corrosion and so its removal makes the object susceptible to further attack of deteriorating factors.

Mechanical Cleaning

Mechanical cleaning refers to dislodge the dirt or corrosion particles by mechanical means and then to remove them. The force required to dislodge encrustations should be more than their force of adhesion of the encrustations to the surface but less than the strength of the object. In order to achieve this, different type of tools are used. Relatively loose encrustations are removed by the use of various types of brushes such as tooth brush and scrubbing brushes. Pointed tools like needle, knife and scalpels can be used for smaller areas of corrosion or encrustation. Dental tools or vibro-tools with suitable abrasive powder are sometimes used for removal of corrosion and other hard encrustations. However, whatever tools are used they should be softer than the metal, for otherwise these may produce scratches on the object.

The advantages of using mechanical methods are that they do not employ any chemical and thus no washing out of the object is required, which is sometimes a very time-consuming process. Mechanical cleaning however, can lead to damage, like scratches and abrasion, if proper care is not taken.

If the metal is soft and fragile and cannot stand to mechanical treatment with hand tools, ultrasonic cleaner can be used. This is an instrument in which sound waves are produced at the bottom of a container which are transferred to the object through the water filled in the container. Since the water having ultrasonic vibrations is responsible for dislodging the encrustations from the object, there is no risk of scratches to the object in such cleaning. Chemical solutions can also be used in this method to soften, dissolve or react with encrustations/corrosion on the object.

Chemical Cleaning

Various chemicals can also be used for the removal of corrosion products from the metals. The selection of chemicals, however, depends upon the type of corrosion to be removed and whether or not patina on the object is to be preserved.

(a) When Patina is to be Sacrificed

If the object is covered by accumulations having malignant corrosion intermixed with it, and there is no other way to save the object from it than to remove the corrosion completely or when some important details or inscriptions on it are hidden under corrosion, the patina has to be sacrificed. Since the complete removal of the patina exposes the metal of the object once again to the environmental factors of deterioration apart from marring the aesthetic beauty of the object, sacrificing the patina is considered to be the last resort and the chemicals used to remove all the traces of corrosion are called stripping agents.

(i) *Alkaline Sodium potassium tatrate (Rochelle salt)*

Object having the corrosion is dipped into the 5% solution of sodium potassium tartrate which has been made alkaline with sodium hydroxide. This treatment removes all the types of corrosion products such as malachite, azurite and atacamite including the noble patina on the surface of the object. Since this is a stripping agent, its concentration should be kept under 5% to avoid too drastic a removal. The chemical treatment should be accompanied with mechanical removal of loosened corrosion.

(ii) *Alkaline Glycerol*

Corrosion products on the objects of copper or its alloys can also be stripped off with the help of a solution of strong alkali containing glycerol. The solution normally used to achieve the purpose with reasonable safety is made of 40g of sodium hydroxide dissolved in one litre of water and adding 40ml of glycerol into it. The softened corrosion is removed from the object mechanically.

(iii) *Sodium hexa meta phosphate (Calagon)*

Sodium hexa meta-phosphate is generally used for the removal of calcareous encrustations on the object and hence is popularly known as cala-gon. However this treatment also converts insoluble cuprous and cupric oxide into soluble cupric phosphate and thus easily removed along with the calcareous deposits. Since oxide is often the first corrosion layer on the surface of the metal objects, all the overlying corrosions could also be brushed off once the oxide becomes loose from the surface. Concentration of the calagon usually used in the solution is 5%.

(iv) *Citric acid*

When two or more objects of copper or its alloys are stuck together because of corrosion products, citric acid has been found to be useful for separating such objects. Such cases are quite common in excavated objects. 2 - 5% hot citric acid is used in such cases. Buffered citric acid has also been used, which is prepared by adding ammonium hydroxide in the solution of citric acid to neutralize it.

(v) *Electrochemical Reduction*

The articles of copper or its alloys can also be made corrosion-free by electrochemical reduction. The object is wrapped with perforated zinc sheet or covered with granulated zinc and immersed in 10% sodium hydroxide solution or in 5% sulphuric acid. Hydrogen produced by the action of sodium hydroxide or sulphuric acid on zinc is responsible for the reduction and thus removal of corrosion. This is a drastic and fast method of removal of corrosion along with its patina, and so it is important to ensure that the object has sufficiently strong metal core present in it or else whole object may crumble into powder.

(vi) *Electrolytic Reduction*

Corrosion on metal objects can also be removed by the process of reduction through the use of electric current. In this process sodium hydroxide, potassium hydroxide or formic acid is used as electrolyte. An iron rod or iron vessel acts as anode while the object itself acts as cathode. When the electric current is passed through the solution acting as electrolyte, hydrogen produced at the anode moves towards the cathode, interacts with the corrosion, reduces and dislodges the corrosion from the surface of the object.

(b) When Patina is to be Retained

Noble patina on old objects in a museum is valued and retained on the object as far as possible. Apart from maintaining the aesthetic beauty of the object, this noble patina isolates the object from the environment and thereby protect it. There are number of methods, which can be used to remove the malignant corrosion while retaining the noble patina.

(i) *Use of hot water*

In this method the object is immersed in hot water for a prolonged period. The corrosion products and other encrustations are softened by hot water, which are removed mechanically from the surface. The tools for mechanical removal of encrustations should be softer than the metal so that these do not produce any scratches on it. This process is slow but it has the of having no after effects of chemical residue as no chemicals are used in the process.

(ii) *Sodium sesquicarbonate solution*

If the object is having 'Bronze disease' and the noble patina on it has to be preserved, then it can be treated with 5-10% solution of sodium sesquicarbonate, which is formed by mixing equal proportion of sodium carbonate and sodium bicarbonate. The object to be treated is immersed in the solution and the softened encrustations and corrosion products are mechanically removed. This treatment converts harmful cuprous chloride to harmless cuprous oxide, which is removed mechanically. Free hydrochloric acid produced in this reaction is neutralized by the alkali of sodium sesquicarbonate. This is a slow process but is safe for the noble pationa.

(iii) *Silver oxide Treatment*

If the malignant bronze disease is present on the object in small patches but the object otherwise is having noble patina free from bronze disease, then instead of exposing the whole object to chemical treatment, the treatment is given only locally. The spots of bronze disease in such cases can be sealed locally with sliver oxide powder. The spots are excavated with the help of pointed metallic tools and the malignant corrosion is mechanically removed as far as possible. The excavated spots are then covered with suspension of silver oxide in alcohol. The object is then placed in humidity chamber and exposed to high humidity for a period of about forty eight hours. Cuprous chloride of the corrosion reacts with silver oxide resulting in the formation of cupric oxide and silver chloride and thereby stops further deterioration due to bronze disease. The process is repeated till there is no appearance of green spots on the object on exposure to high humidity.

(iv) *Use of Benzotriazole (BTA)*

Solution of Benzotriazole in alcohol can be used to inhibit the corrosion on copper objects. It was recommended to impregnate the object under vacuum in 3% solution of BTA in methylated spirit. Standard method of using BTA is to first degrease the object with acetone followed by its immersing in 3% alcholic solution. Vacaum is created to remove air bubbles from the surface of metal and to ensure close contact of BTA with the surface. Vacuum is continued till the bulbbles cease to evolve. The object is then removed from the bath and rinsed with methylated spirit to remove the excess of BTA. It is then dried and given a surface coating containing BTA. While using this method, care may be taken to avoid inhaling the fine powder of BTA and also its contact with the skin by using rubber or polythene gloves.

BTA being toxic in nature, a number of variations in the use of BTA have been used. The most common is the replacement of methylated spirit with water. 1% aqueous suspention of BTA at room temperature has been found to be quite effective. BTA can act as vapour inhibitor as well, and is also effective when the object is wrapped in the paper impregnated with 0.5-2% suspension of BTA in water.

Whatever chemical method is used for the removal of corrosion, it is extremely important to wash off the residual chemicals completely. Any residual chemical used may lead to further corrosion of the object. It may take several days for complete removal depending upon the chemical to be removed and the condition of the object. After ensuring that the object is free from any residual chemical, it is dried at a temperature of about 60 degree Celsius and given a preservative coating of polyvinyl acetate, polymethylmeth acrylate or paraloid B72 in a suitable volatile solvent.

5

Miniature Paintings of the Assamese Manuscript

Samiran Boruah

The manuscript writing is a very old tradition of Assam. It is known from Bāṇabhaṭṭa's *Harṣacarita,* belonging to seventh century AD that the gift from Bhāskarabarman, the king of ancient Assam, to Harṣavardhana included, inter alia, "volumes of fine writing with leaves made from aloe bark and of the hue of ripe pink cucumber." It is also known from Bāṇa's account that in Assam there was a tradition of painting miniature pictures. But there is no clear indication about illustrated manuscripts in his account. Most of the scholars on Indian art believe that it is only from the sixteenth century that the Hindus started illustrating their manuscripts, long after the Buddhists and the Jains. But it is discovered from recent investigation that there was a Hindu tradition of manuscript illustration in Nepal as early as the twelfth century AD. So the existence of such a Hindu tradition in Assam in an earlier date cannot be ruled out.

One of the most significant things about the Assamese manuscripts is that the calligraphic elegance was considered to be important part of it. As a result, four stylistically distinct types of Assamese scripts have evolved in different Assamese manuscripts. They were *Gargaiyan, Bamunia, Lahkari* and

Kaithali. In this context it may be mentioned that in rest of India it is only from the eighteenth century, that too under the direct influence of the Mughal court, that the Hindus have taken the calligraphic excellence seriously.

The study of the Assamese painted manuscripts reveals that there existed two distinct schools of paintings in Assam. Most of the paintings of the seventeenth century can be grouped together on the basis of their common features and they share some of the characteristics with the early western Indian tradition. Regarding the *Bhāgavata* of Bali Satra, a well- known Assamese illustrated manuscript, which shows similar characteristics with the above group of manuscripts, Moti Chandra ("Reviews" in the *Journal of the University of Gauhati*, vol. V, 1954) remarked that the paintings of the Bali *Satra Bhāgavata* are similar to the Nepalese scroll and the Bengal paintings of the eighteenth century. However, so far documented paintings of the above group will prove Moti Chandra's view to be wrong. A comparison with some of the published eighteenth century Nepalese and Bengali paintings show that the Assamese paintings are closer to the fifteenth and sixteenth century North Indian tradition rather than to the eighteenth century paintings of Nepal and Bengal. It may be pointed out here that many scholars believe that the North Indian style of painting have originated from the Western Indian tradition. Karl J. Khandalavala and Moti Chandra had opined that the Western Indian or Gujarati school was not a localized mode of expression confined only to Gujarat, Rajasthan, Malwa and Jaunpur but had become a form of expression common to many parts of India (*New Document of Indian Paintings*, Prince of Wales Museum). The exact structural similarities of the compositions of some of the Assamese paintings of the above group with that of the *Laur-Chanda* (1450-1475 AD) and *Mrigavat* (1525-1570 AD) of Bharat Kala Bhavan proves beyond doubt that they have originated from the same tradition. But at the same time, some of the most conspicuous peculiarities of the Assamese paintings prove that the Assamese school had originated before the Persian influence became perceptible in North India.

It is very significant that Bāṇa in his *Harṣacarita* has mentioned that the gifts from Bhāskaravarman, the seventh century king of Kāmarūpa (present day Assam) to King Harṣa had included a pair of wooden panels, to one side of which were attached colour pots of small gourds and brushes. There could be only one interpretation for the existence of these, – that they were definitely used for painting the miniatures. It proves that there was a tradition of miniature paintings in Assam as early as the seventh century AD. It is curious that most of the scholars of Indian paintings have so far evaded such an interpretation.

The documented seventeenth century manuscripts are undoubtedly the remnants of an old tradition. Some of the similarities of the Assamese paintings with those of the Western Indian and the Northern Indian schools may indicate that a more or less common style was popular in many parts of India during the seventh century AD.

It is possible to compare a few more manuscripts of North India with the seventeenth century paintings of Assam. In the *Āraṇyaka Parvan* (1516 AD), we find that the compositions are often stacked in several panels, one on top of the other in the same folio. In some of the Assamese paintings too, we find several panels in the same folio, though not in an exact fashion. Besides, the depiction of the four headed Brahmā is similar in both the manuscripts. The *Mahāpurāṇa* from Palam (1540 AD) also share some common features with the Assamese paintings. Besides the similar palette, the almost identical male costume and the conventional ways of depicting the plants and animals are quite remarkable. In an early *Rāgamālā* of Bhārat Kalā Bhavan (1575 AD), we come across similar male costume. The turban depicted in this *Rāgamālā* is an indication that the so-called Akbari *atpati* turban, which abounds in Assamese paintings and which most of the scholars want to associate with the Mughal school has really been in existence in Indian art prior to the existence of the Mughal school. This view is further substantiated by the presence of an *atpati* type turban in Sunga sculpture, the photograph of which was reproduced by Moti Chandra (*Prācīn Bhārat Kī Veśbhūṣā,* Bharati Bhandar, Prayag). Norman Brown also reproduced a photograph of the eleventh century sculpture bearing three male figures, two of which were shown with turbans exactly similar to the so-called *atpati* turban ("Early Vaiṣṇava Miniature paintings from Western India," *Eastern Art,* vol. 11, 1930).

Most of the scholars who have discussed about the Assamese manuscript paintings want to associate the turban of the Assamese paintings with the Mughal paintings. But they fail to see that except the turban no other element of the Assamese paintings can be even remotely associated with the Mughal School. Conversely, there are many elements in the Assamese paintings, which are not found in the Mughal School or in the late Rajasthani School. Those who are really aware about the workings of the influences in the art forms will agree that it is not just simply picking up an element or two from the foreign source. In this case it is even more absurd to assume that the Assamese painters have chosen just the turban, which is quite insignificant visually or from pictorial perspective, and ignored all the rich and fabulous attributes of the Mughal School.

The convention of the Assamese paintings of placing figures under arched canopies is also leading many scholars to wrong conclusions. They want to associate this tradition with the Buddhist paintings of the Pāla School. But this convention also exists in the Western Indian tradition. In the manuscript of the *Sārdhaśataka* (c.1125-1150 AD) and the *Mahāpurāṇa* from Palam (1540 AD), similar arched canopies are noticed. It is also noteworthy that we find similar convention in some rock-cut sculptures of Assam belonging to the tenth and eleventh centuries AD. On the other hand, the canopies are not always arched in the Assamese paintings. In many cases they are angular, forming step-like pattern. In other cases, the canopies are rudimentary and exist just as a decorative element rather than a device for providing niches over the figures.

It can be presumed that even though the above mentioned documented manuscripts have been done in seventeenth century, they really represent a very older tradition which is closer to the Western Indian tradition. This can be further supported by the existence of a particular manuscript, namely *Anādipatan*. This manuscript is probably produced towards the end of the seventeenth century or early eighteenth century. In this manuscript, we find quite a good number of abstract paintings. This is quite unique in the sense that nowhere in India similar abstract visualization is found except in the illustrations of the Jain manuscript, the-*Trailokya dipikā* with which it shares some remote connection. Both these manuscripts deal with the cosmology. But the illustrations of the *Trailokya-dipikā* are more like geometrical drawings lacking any organic and visual quality. In contrast, the illustrations of the *Anādipatan* are quite organic and exceptionally rich in pictorial quality enabling them to stand independently without the aid of their intended significance. But it is remarkable that both the Jaina and the Assamese manuscripts belonging to two different areas separated by a vast geographical expanse, deal with the same subject and in both cases, the illustrations are abstract in nature. Absence of any such manuscript in the adjacent areas in between them, indirectly points to a very remote common tradition which has been destroyed in the turbulent North-Central India and had only survived in two extreme edges of the country

The characteristics of the Assamese paintings of the seventeenth century can be listed as follows:

1. The general composition consists of a large central

area, generally painted red, where the subjects are depicted and a narrow surrounding border in green or blue, broader at the top, forming a series of canopies over the central area. There is no attempt to differentiate the various planes. Though red is used as background colour almost everywhere, yet yellow, pink and blue are also used in exceptional cases.

2. The male and female figures are always conventional and except in the portrayal of Brahmā, all figures are depicted in profile.
3. The male costume consists of a *dhoti* and a scarf hanging from the neck with its two ends freely falling over the shoulders on either side. The female costume consists of a *mekhalā* (long skirt) and a *rihā* (scarf) tied round the waist and bosom that runs further behind to cover the hair knot forming a balloon like appearance.
4. The male head gear consists of three-pointed or four-pointed tiara in some cases or else the *atpati* type turban.
5. The treatment of the landscape is always conventional. Water is always painted in a basket of square or rectangular pattern. Trees are generally painted like the sprays. The mountains are depicted as piles of multicoloured convex bodies.
6. Depiction of animals and birds are both conventional and naturalistic.
7. The architecture is very simple consisting of cross section view of the Assam type houses with roofs and supporting pillars. In many cases, instead of drawing the complete house, simply the door or a single pillar is depicted independently.
8. The umbrella is mostly depicted as hanging from a hook like handle.

The documented manuscripts belonging to the

eighteenth century forms a style in which the seventeenth century elements as well as the Rajput-Mughal elements have been found to converge in a unique manner. The flavour of the Rajput-Mughal idiom when translated from its vertical format to the horizontal format of the Assamese manuscript and being blended with the local idioms, naturally resulted in a unique style. In this group of manuscripts, green seems to have replaced red as the background colour. Besides, many new shades of colour hitherto unknown to the Assamese painters began to appear in most of the paintings.

The seventeenth century convention of dividing the composition into the central area and surrounding border is almost abandoned in this group of paintings. But here, an attempt to differentiate the various planes of the composition can be noticed distinctly. But in spite of this effort of defining perspective, most of the paintings lack the depth that is found in the Rajput-Mughal idioms. However, the solidity of the body is fairly achieved in the depiction of male and female figures. The male and female faces are depicted in different ways. Some are depicted in profile, some in three-quarter and others in their frontal view. The costume, particularly those of the female became very elaborate and in many cases they became identical with the costume of late Rajasthani paintings.

The plants and animals in this group of manuscripts are both conventional and naturalistic. Great varieties of flowering trees are found in some of the manuscripts of this group. They are quite unique and are depicted in ornamented decorative pattern rather than like natural plants. The depiction of the hills and mountains are also different from the seventeenth century manuscripts.

The architectural depiction is quite complex with borrowing elements from the Rajput-Mughal paintings. There are also instances where a new type of architecture has been found to have evolved from such borrowing. But there are also instances where, instead of the complete building, simply the door is depicted, following the seventeenth century convention.

The chariots are depicted in many ways. In some cases there are simple platforms mounted on four wheels and sometimes they are elaborately decorated and are mounted on two wheels. There are canopies overhead in some of them while in others there are no such canopies. The umbrella is differently depicted in this group from that of the seventeenth century hanging type.

The main purpose of the traditional paintings of Assam was to supplement the text of the manuscripts. In other words they were the illustrations of the texts. As such these artists were basically concerned on the contents of the texts. So instead of creating new meaning with form and colour, they were contented with the already existing meanings of the texts. It is now hard to detect how much the artists were inspired even by the text itself as in most cases artists' job was just to copy them from other manuscripts. There was a special class of people in Assam known as *khanikars.* They were both artists and the craftsmen. Besides paintings they also made wooden idols. It may be pointed out here that the word *pratimā* was applied indiscriminately to both sculptures and paintings. *Khanikars* used to make masks for theatrical performances.

The scribe of the manuscript was usually a different person called *lekhaka.* Generally he did the writing first and left blank spaces to be filled with illustrations later by the *khanikars.* But *lekhakas* were invariably literate persons whereas *khanikars* were mostly illiterate. But they could copy paintings as well as writings. So it is obvious that sometimes *khanikars* did their job without fully understanding the essence of the text. But as all the themes of the manuscripts were part of the general folklore tradition of Assam, the *khanikars* were not totally unfamiliar with them. However such factors were also responsible to some extent in determining the nature and characteristics of the traditional Assamese paintings.

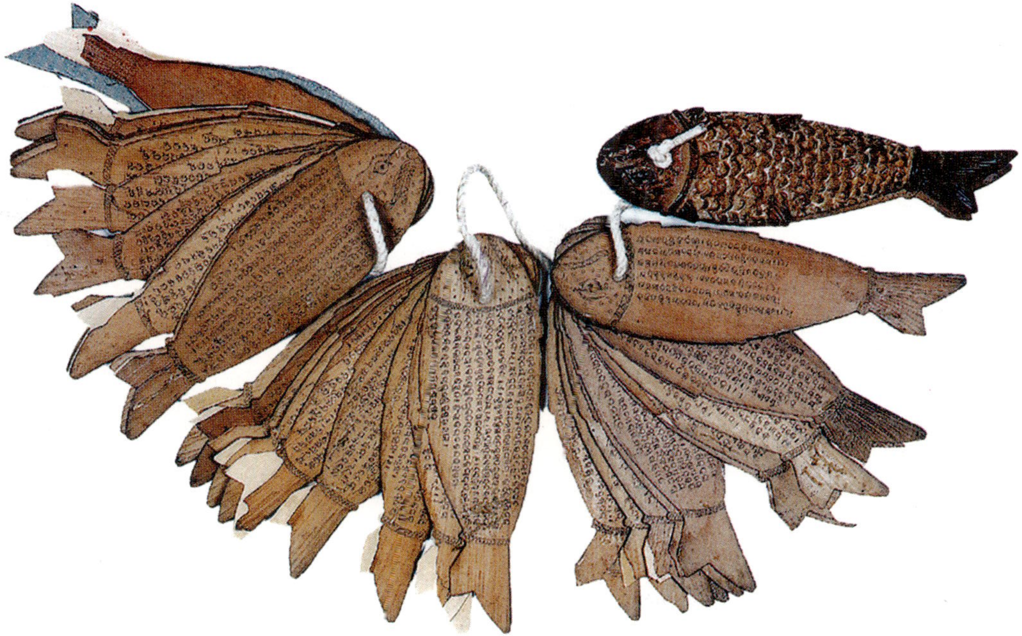

Plate 1. Fish shaped folios of manuscripts on palm leaves

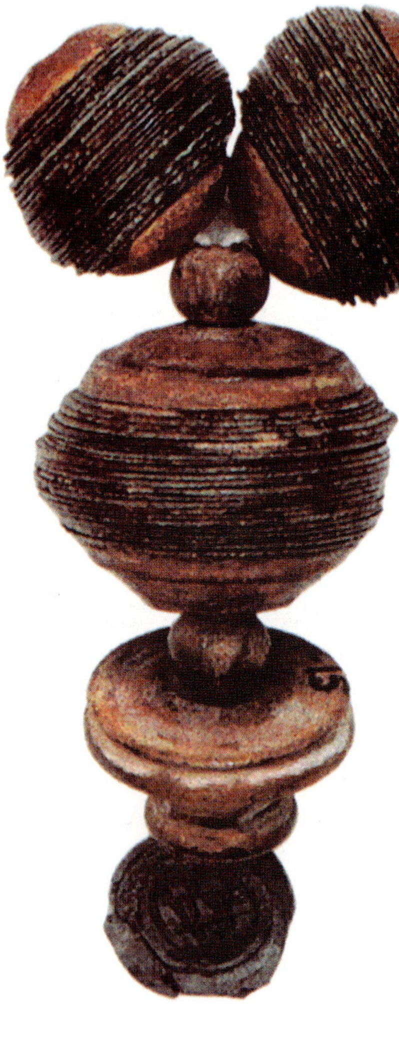

Plate 2. Round shaped folios of manuscripts on palm leaves between wooden covers

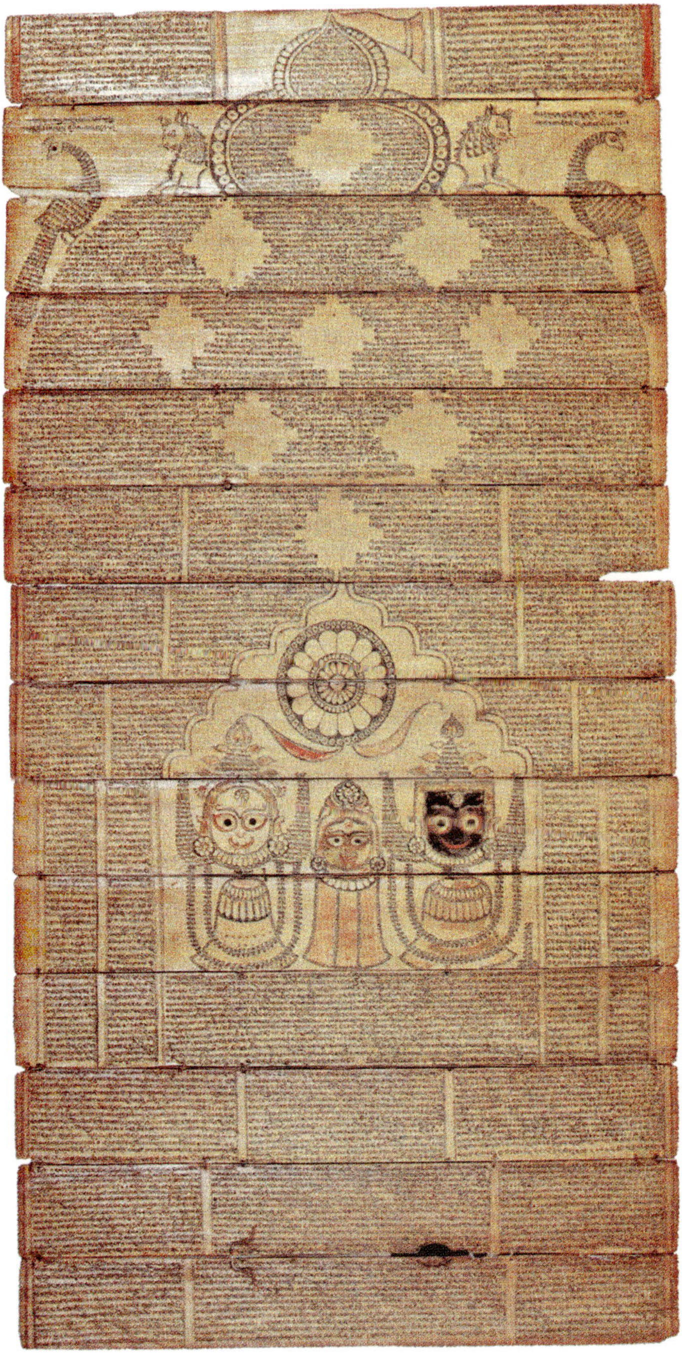

Plate 3. Illustrated manuscript folio on palm leaves stitched together to have a bigger Format

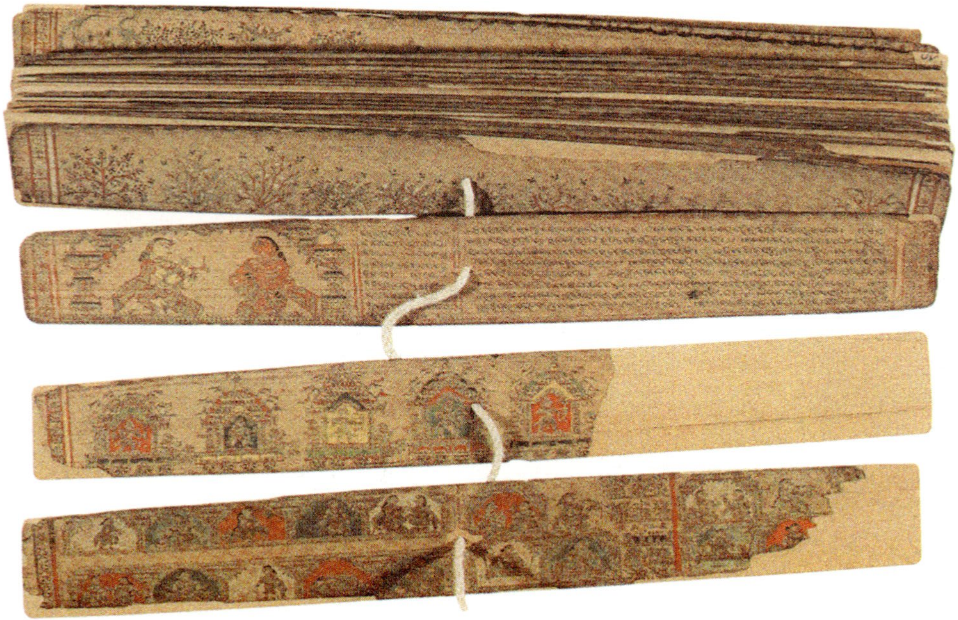

Plate 4. Folios of an illustrated manuscript on palm leaves, after restoration

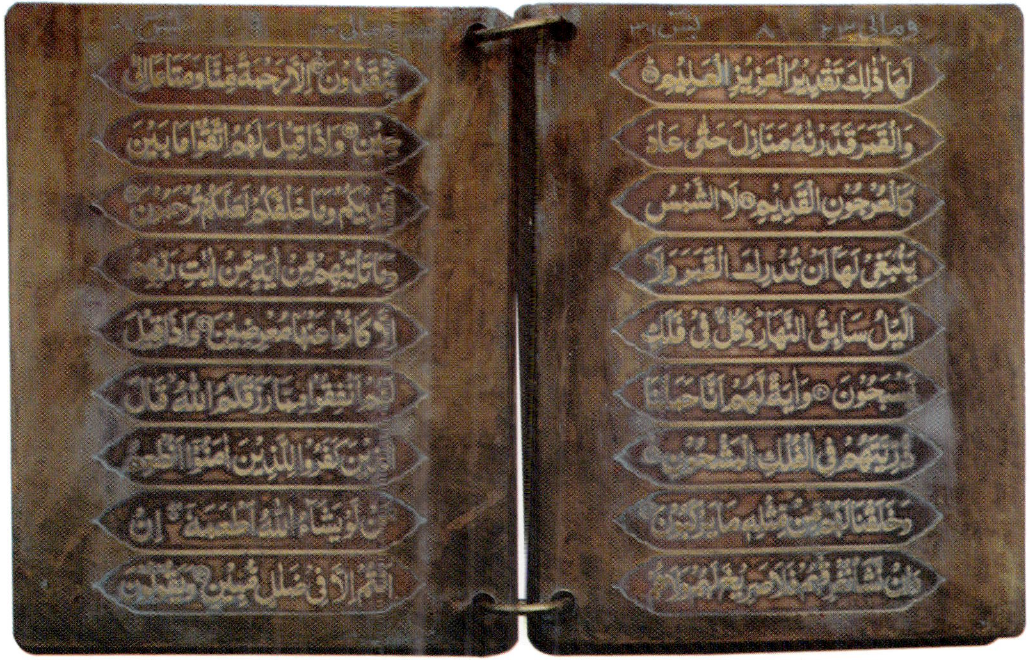

Plate 5. Manuscript on metal sheet

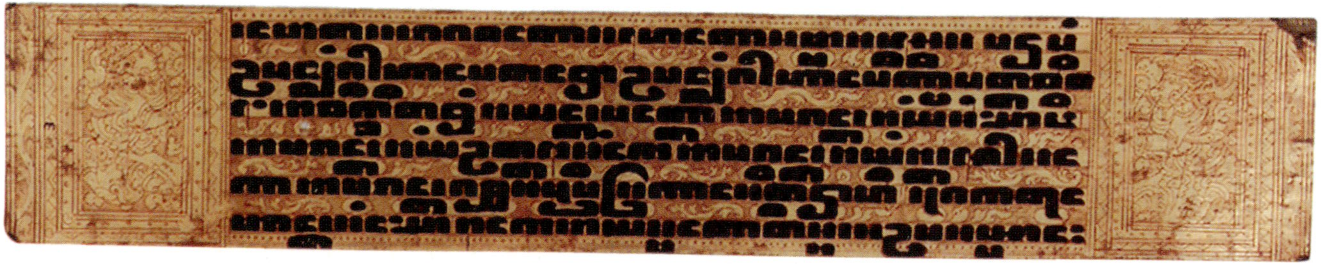

Plate 6. Manuscript and illustration on copper sheet

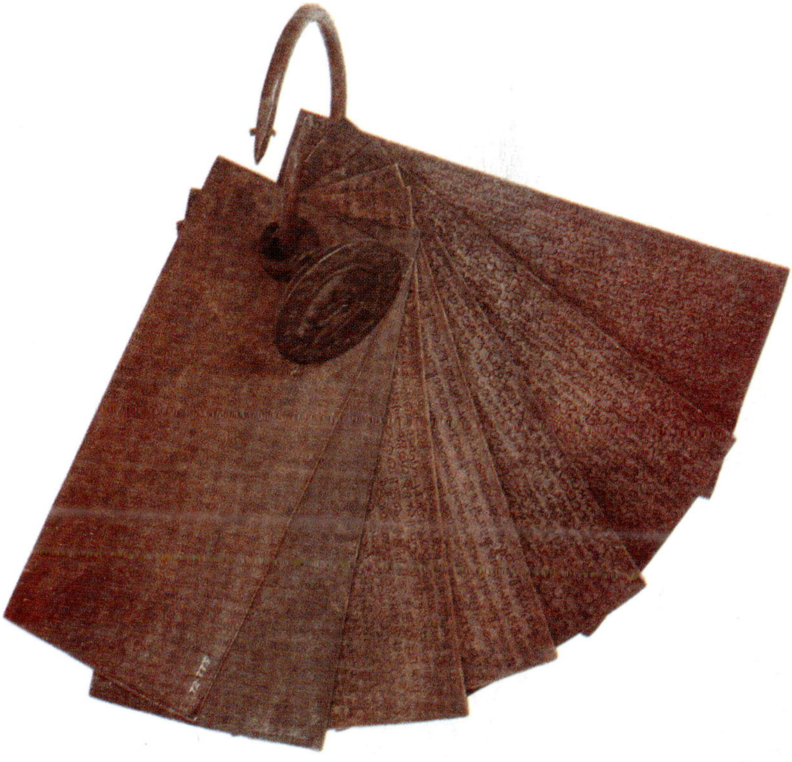

Plate 7. Manuscript folios on copper alloy bound together with metal ring

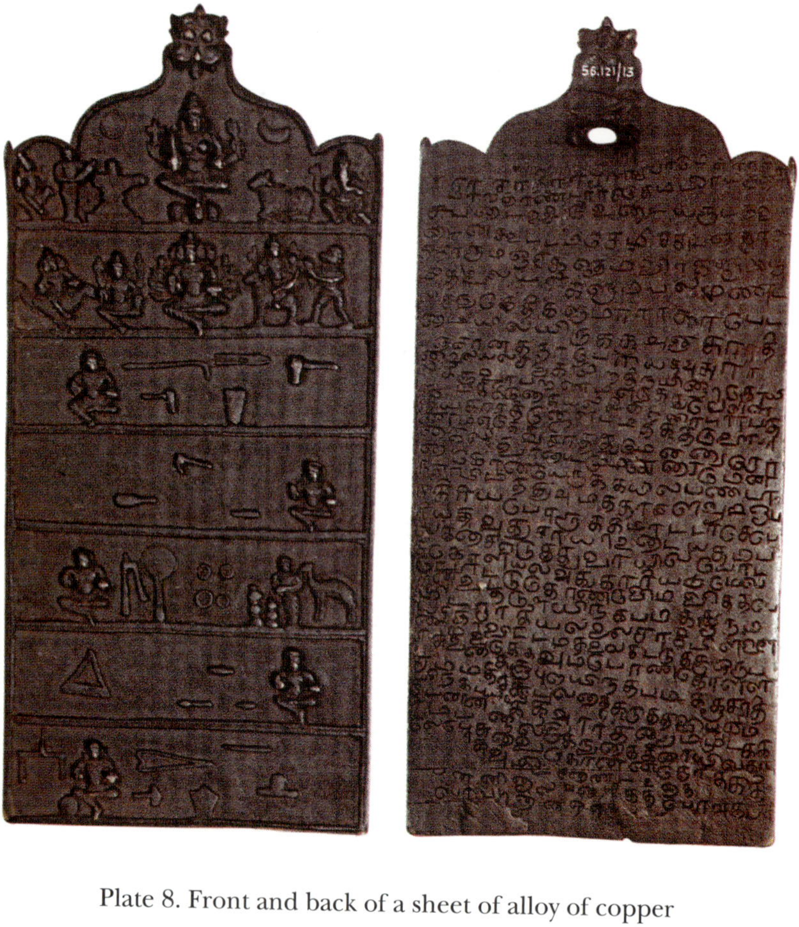

Plate 8. Front and back of a sheet of alloy of copper

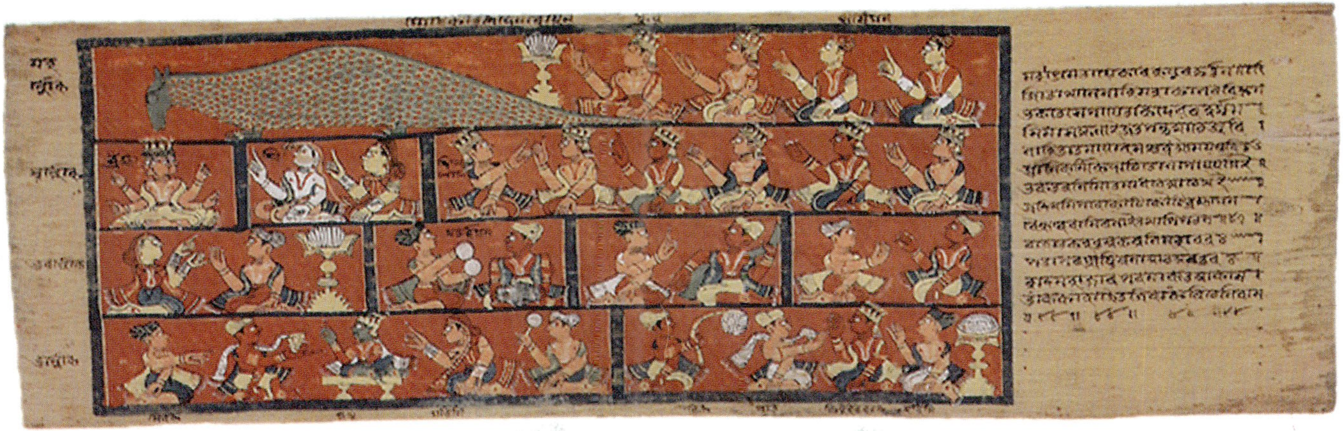

Plate 9. Asamese miniature painting on *sanchipat*

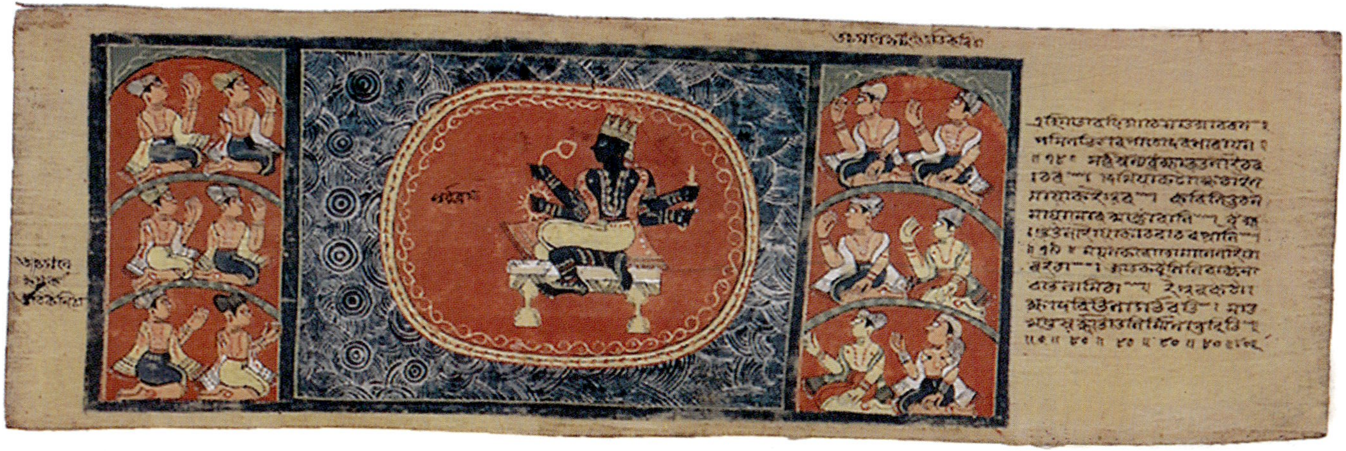

Plate 10. Asamese miniature painting on *sanchipat*

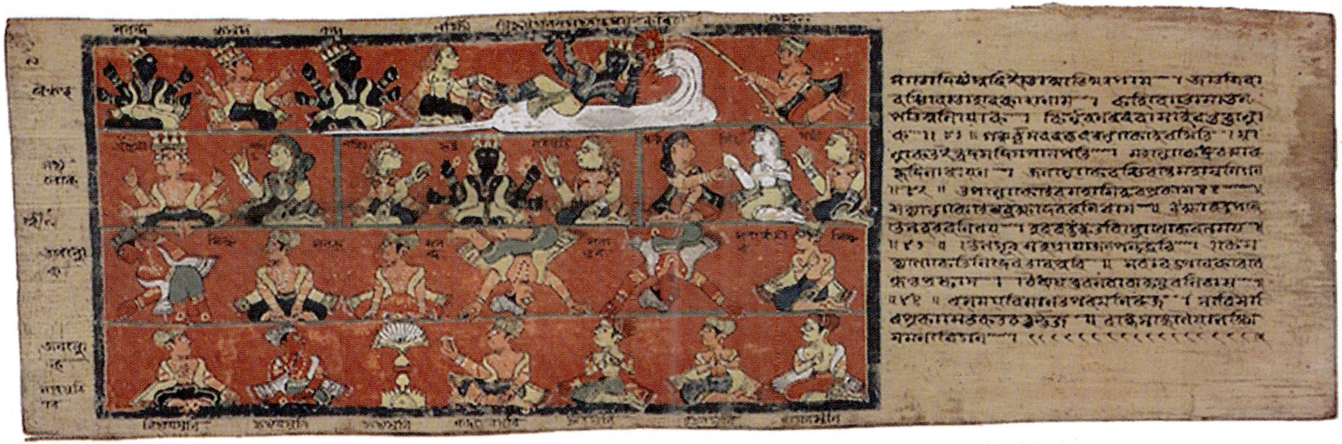

Plate 11. Asamese miniature painting on *sanchipat*

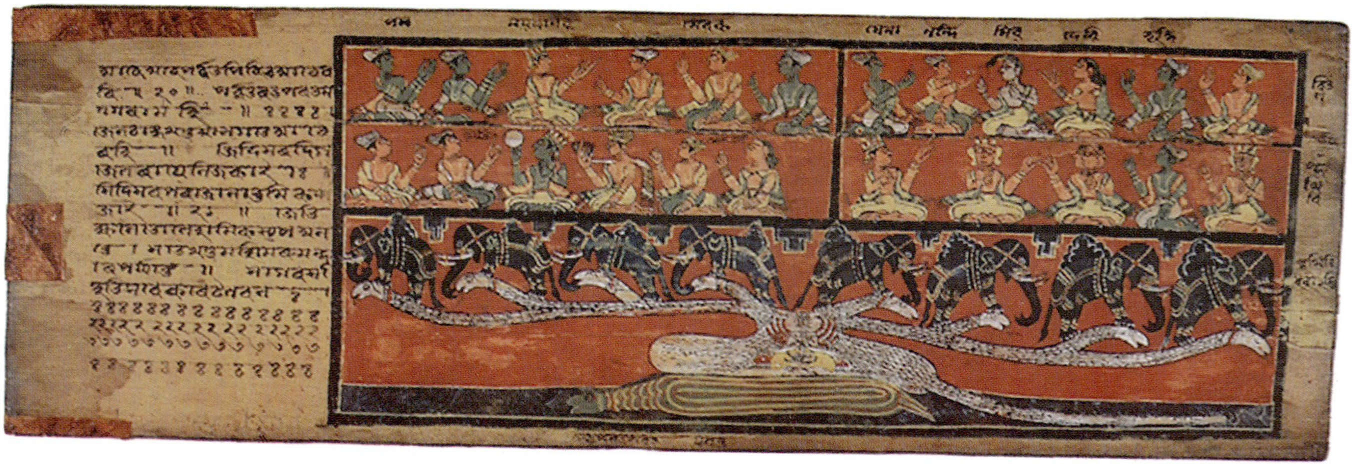

Plate 12. Asamese miniature painting on *sanchipat*

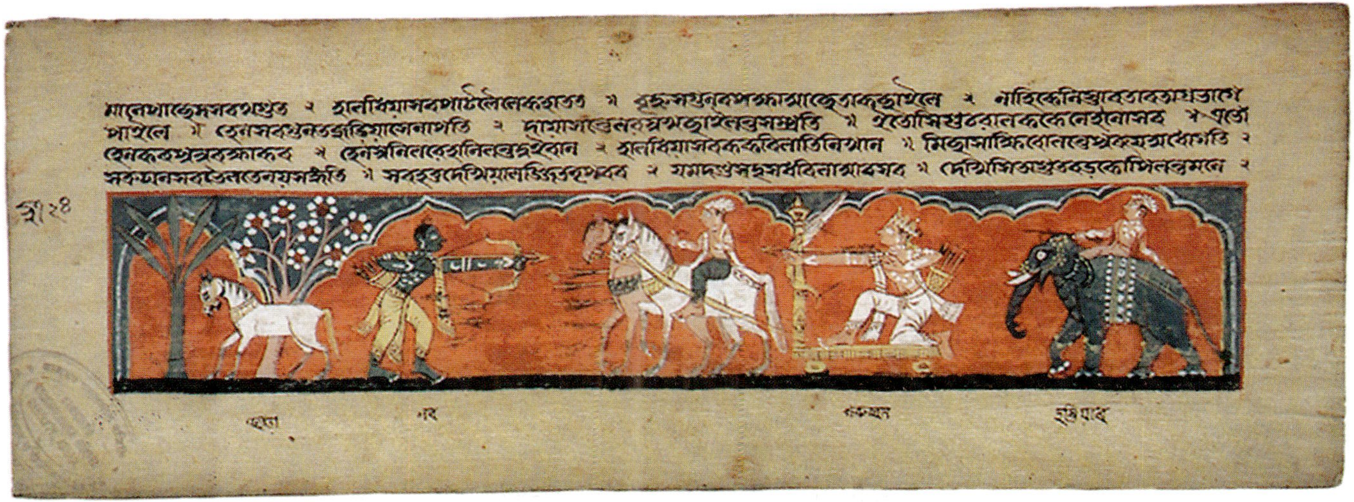

Plate 13. Illustrated manuscript folio on *sanchipat*

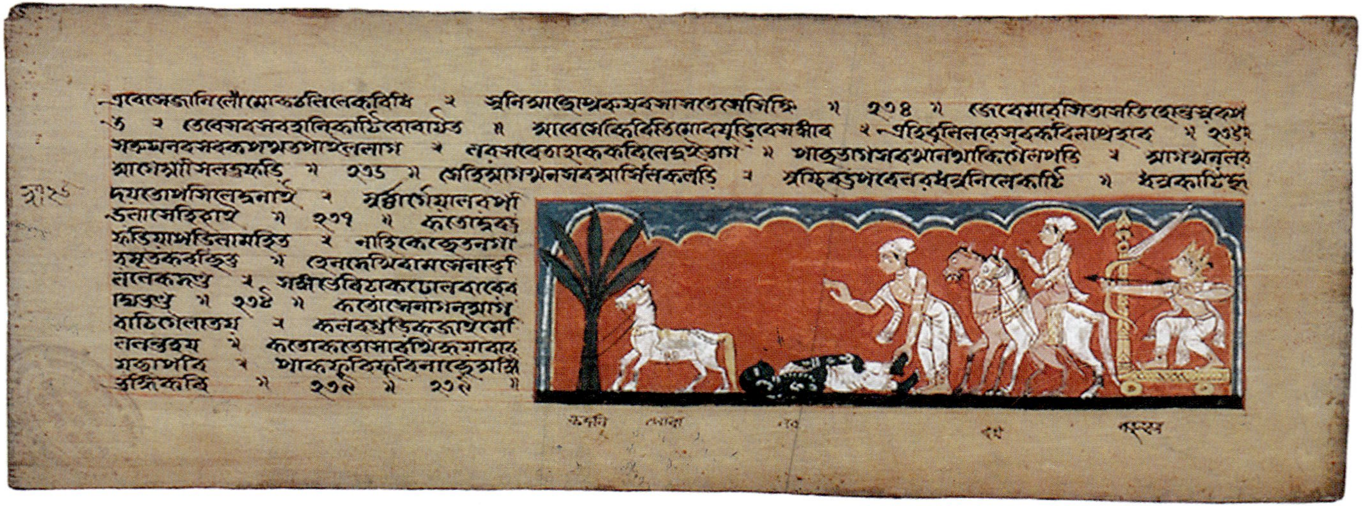

Plate 14. Illustrated manuscript folio on *sanchipat*

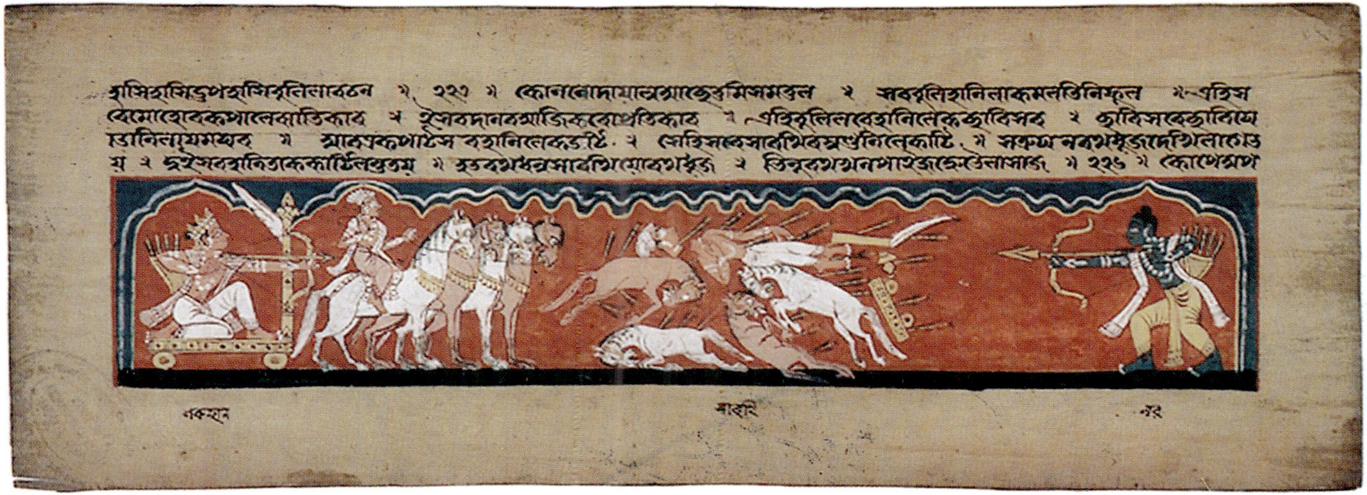

Plate 15. Illustrated manuscript folio on *sanchipat*

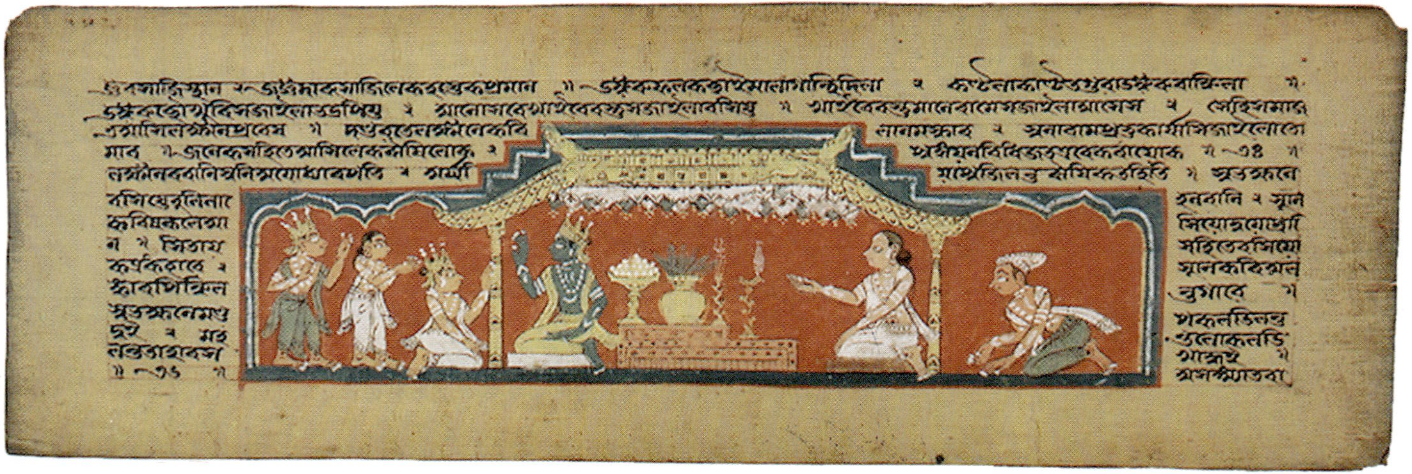

Plate 16. Illustrated manuscript folio on *sanchipat*

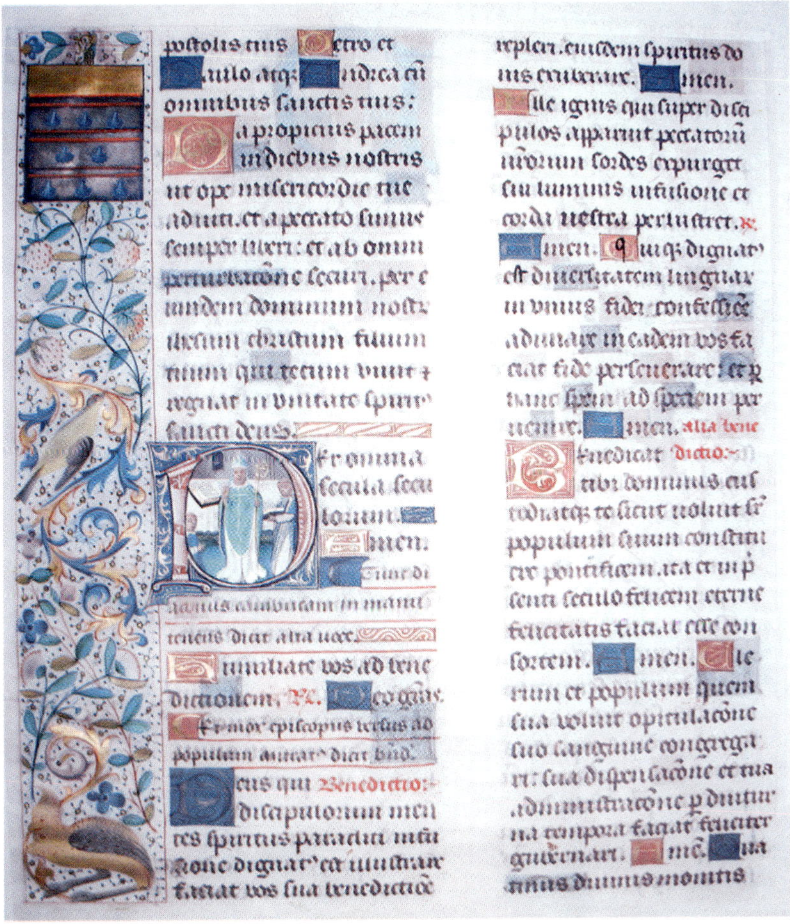

Plate 17. Folio of a manuscript on parchment from the collection of National Museum, New Delhi (Courtesy National Museum, New Delhi)

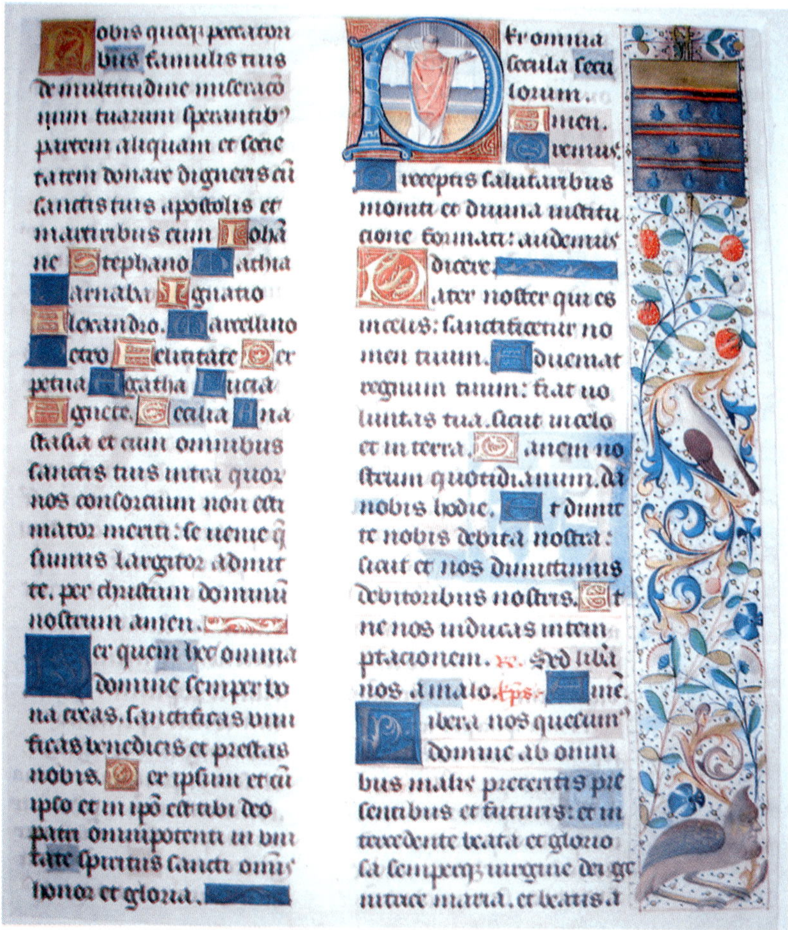

Plate 18. Folio of a manuscript on parchment from the collection of National Museum, New Delhi
(Courtesy National Museum, New Delhi)

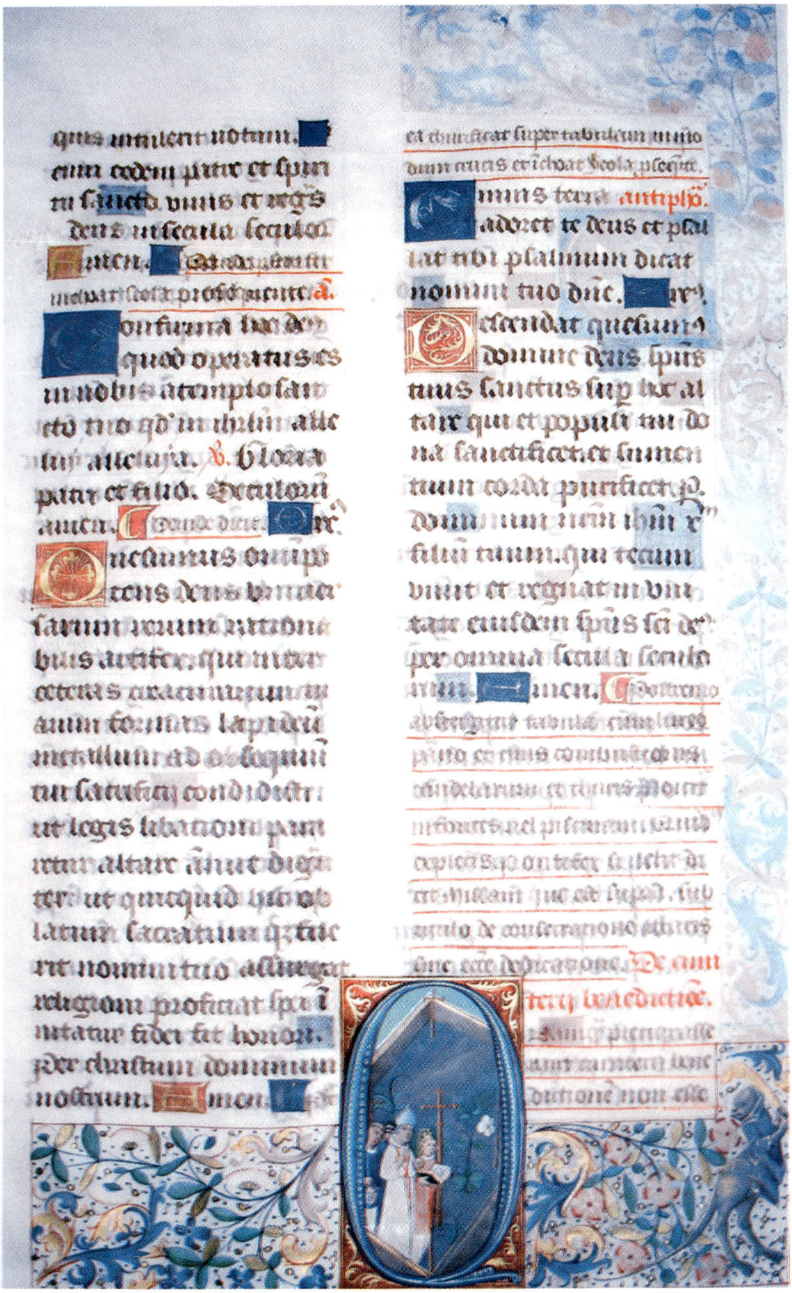

Plate 19. Folio of a manuscript on parchment from the collection of National Museum, New Delhi
(Courtesy National Museum, New Delhi)

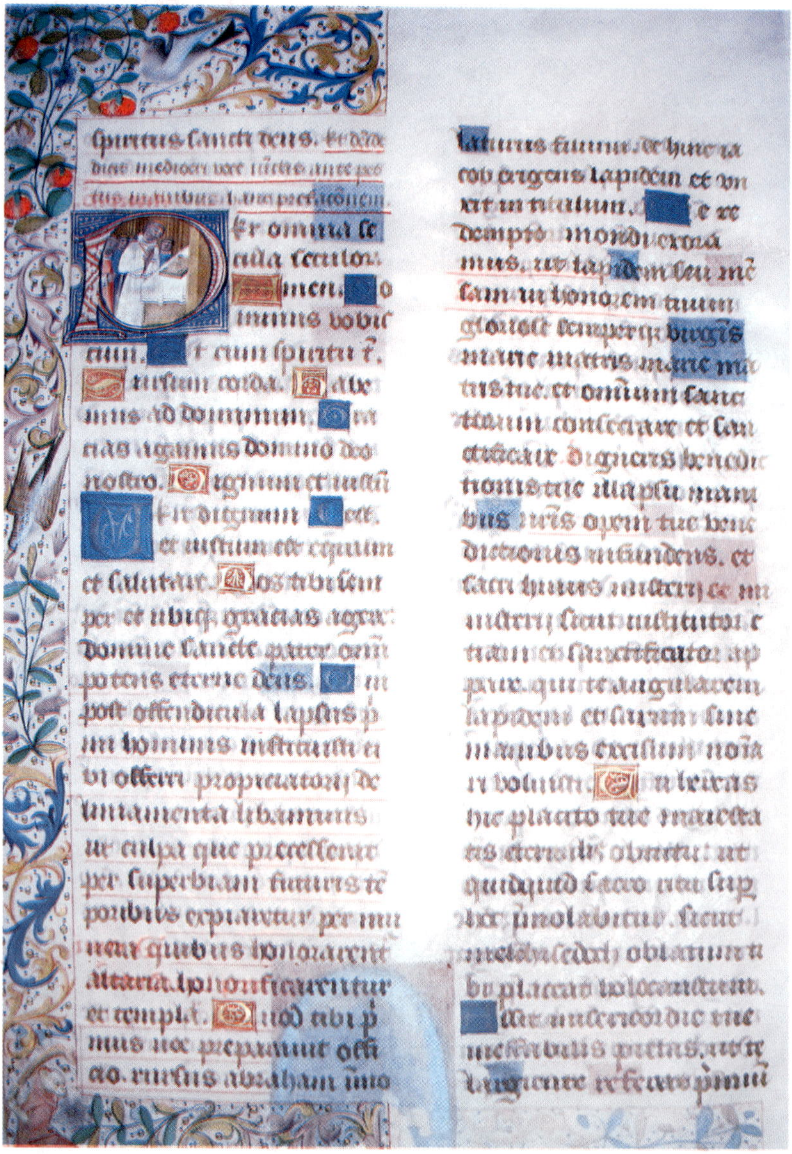

Plate 20. Folio of a manuscript on parchment from the collection of National Museum, New Delhi
(Courtesy National Museum, New Delhi)

It is quite obvious from the above facts that one cannot appreciate the Assamese manuscript painting wholeheartedly without knowing the accompanying texts of the manuscript. It is the text which has relevance to the paintings though the Assamese manuscript paintings have an indigenous beauty. Its beauty derives basically from its uniqueness and the provincial flavour of simplicity. When we compare the Assamese paintings with those of the schools of late Rajasthani, Kangra, Mughal, etc., which are basically the products of urban cultures, we notice the uniqueness of the Assamese paintings, primarily as a product of the village culture. Though some kings and queens of the late mediaeval Assam used to commission scribes and painters to prepare manuscripts, yet there is no evidence to think that they had their own royal ateliers. Manuscripts were generally prepared by the traditional scribes and painters who lived in the villages. It may be pointed out that the materials for the Assamese manuscripts were mainly prepared from the bark of the Agar tree which is found only in the countryside. As the painters and scribes used to prepare the base materials for the manuscripts themselves, which involved a very long and laborious process, it was advantageous for them to do the work there itself. Besides, painting had never been a viable profession in Assam. The traditional painters known as *khanikars* had to depend for their livelihood, basically on farming. So it was not possible for him to settle in urban centres near his clients to do the paintings exclusively. The Vaiṣṇava monasteries, another site for the production of manuscripts, were also situated away from the urban area. The seclusion of the traditional painters was a determining factor in shaping the style of the Assamese paintings. It also helped to retain the characteristics, perhaps, of a very old tradition which had been abandoned elsewhere in India long before.

6

Conservation of *Sanchipat* Manuscripts

K.K. Gupta

BEFORE THE advent of paper in India, various kinds of plant materials were used for writing purposes, depending upon their availability in different areas. *Sanchipat* was one such material used in North-eastern states of the country, such as Assam, Tripura and Meghalaya. *Sanchipat* was made out of the bark of agar wood tree (*Aquilaria agallocha*).

The exact date of introduction of Agar bark as writing material is not known. As regards the specific use of agar bark, several authentic *sanchipat* specimens of the seventeenth century are available in different collections in the North-eastern states.

Making of Sanchipat Manuscripts

Sanchipat sheets used to be made from the raw bark of agar tree by a complex process consisting of curing, seasoning and polishing. The freshly prepared *sanchipat* sheet has a pale yellow appearance, which gets darker with age. Each strip of the bark of the tree was rolled with its outer or greener surface inside and dried in sun for several days. They were then rubbed by hand to remove the outer scaly portion of the bark. They were exposed to dew for one night and the next morning outer layer of the bark was carefully removed and the strips were cut into sheets of convenient sizes varying from twenty-five to sixty cm in length and eight to twenty cm in width. The sheets were then put in cold water to remove all water soluble material, followed by smoothening with a knife. A paste of *Matimah* tree (*Phaseolus raditus*) gum was rubbed over the sheets, which were then treated with *harital* (orpiment). This treatment made the sheets smoother and immune to insect attack. The sheets were finally dried in sun and rubbed with smooth stone or conch shell. Carbon ink as well as iron gall ink was used for writing purposes on these *sanchipat* sheets.

The illustrations on these sheets were strictly confined to a specific area of the sheet called '*ālekhya sthāna.*' (place for writing) *Kharimatti* (mainly calcium carbonate), *hingul* (vermilion), *harital* (orpiment), red ochre, yellow ochre, indigo, lac red and lampblack were the main pigments used for illustrations and the binding medium was the gum of locally available trees .

Deterioration

The factors responsible for the deterioration of *sanchipat* manuscripts can be broadly classified into two main categories:

External factors

- Humidity
- Temperature
- Light
- Pollution
- Biological growth
- Mechanical causes

Internal factors

- Constituents of *sanchipat*
- Technique of making the manuscripts

The deterioration of *sanchipat* manuscripts is the cumulative effect of all these deteriorating factors. Their damage is more or less similar to those of palm leaf manuscripts. They lose their flexibility with age because of the polymerization of the natural oil present in them and to some extent due to the heat and environmental conditions. Because of their brittleness they tend to get damaged from their edges and at the holes meant for passing string to bind them. As in all types of wood, the material of *sanchipat* is anisotropic in nature, i.e. it expands and contracts differently in different directions with changes in relative humidity, resulting in its cracking and warping. This occurence of warping is also because of its tendency to revert to its original curvilinear shape of the bark of trees.

In case of illustrated manuscripts, the main support of *sanchipat* and the paint layer of the illustrations have different expansion and contraction due to the changes in relative humidity, and thus cause the cracking and flaking of paint layer.

Conservation

Conservation of *sanchipat* manuscripts can be classified into Preventive Conservation and Curative Conservation.

Preventive Conservation

Preventive Conservation is the control of factors of deterioration responsible for the decay of manuscripts. It basically involves control of environmental and other external mechanical factors of deterioration. It does not involve any interaction with the manuscript as such, and that is why it is often called Passive conservation. This type of conservation is very useful and fulfils one of the main precepts of the ethics of conservation —minimum interaction with the objects.

Moisture present in the atmosphere plays an important role in the deterioration of manuscripts of all types.

Recommended limits of temperature and Relative Humidity in the area having the collection of *sanchipat* manuscripts are 20°C-25°C and 45%-55% respectively without sharp fluctuations even between these limits.

Light is essential for reading a manuscript, but is also a very potent factor of its deterioration. *Sanchipat* manuscripts, being organic in nature are susceptible to damage by light. Since the extent of damage depends upon the intensity, proportion of Ultra Violet radiations present in it and the period of exposure, all these factors need to be minimized to avoid its damage by light. Recommended upper limit of intensity of light for sensitive materials such as *sanchipat* is 50 lux. Furthermore, the manuscripts should not be exposed to light unnecessarily and light should preferably be free from Ultra Violet radiations, as far as possible.

Environmental pollution, because of the acidic gases and the suspended particulate matter is also a source of damage to manuscripts. This can be controlled at source by taking suitable measures like using sulphur-free fuel and installing pollution-control devices in factories, powerhouses and means of transportation. This effort can be reinforced by supplementary measures; for example, developing green belts around the repositories having manuscript collections. Wrapping the manuscripts in starch-free cloth also protects them from pollution. Since no such method is foolproof, all possible actions should be taken simultaneously.

Bio-deterioration is not a significant problem in case of Sanchipat, because the wood of agar tree from which these are made, is resistant to insect attack. During their making by traditional method, the use of orpiment, while serving the purpose of giving them a coating, makes them poisonous and so immune to insect attack. The control of temperature and RH also helps keeping the insects away.

Curative Conservation

If the damage has already occurred to the manuscripts,

curative operations are undertaken to undo the damage and bring the manuscripts back to their original condition, as far as possible. All such operations taken together are called Curative Conservation. The cleaning, flattening and reinforcement are three main operations in curative conservation of *Sanchipat* manuscripts.

Cleaning

Loose dust and dirt and other incrustations on the *sanchipat* sheets can be removed mechanically by the use of dry brush, erasers or fine scalpels. Hard or stubborn incrustations can sometimes be softened by the use of solvents or water depending upon the nature of incrustation and then be removed mechanically. Excessive water should be avoided, as it may result in its cracking and warping. In case, water is used for cleaning or for softening of some incrustations on the manuscript folios, these should be dried fast. Water should preferably be used in combination with alcohol so that it dries fast.

Flattening

Warped sheets can be flattened by putting them under pressure after their humidification. The pressure could be created manually or by vacuum on a vacuum table. Pressure should be gradually increased and suitable padding be provided to the leaves to avoid any cracking of the brittle leaves. The sheets when completely dried are placed between the cover boards and tied tightly with fastening string. These should always be covered with de-starched cotton cloth in order to protect the folios of manuscript from the fluctuations of humid conditions.

Reinforcement

Reinforcement is strengthening of torn or weakened support. Tears and holes etc. in the *sanchipat* should be repaired as soon as these are noticed. These tend to increase during handling if timely repair is not undertaken.

When there is no loss of material at the tears, they can be joined by applying an adhesive just at their edges. Sometimes, the edges of the tear (slanting tear) have sufficient area for application of adhesive and a strong joint can be achieved. In case the tear is straight, a thin tissue paper strip can be stuck at the back of the tear to give additional strength to the joint. It is advisable to chamfer the edges of the strip to avoid any abrupt change in thickness of the *sanchipat* sheet. The losses in *sanchipat* support can be restored by using pieces of blank *sanchipat* sheet, similar in thickness and strength. Wheat starch or flour paste or carboxy methyl cellulose can be used as adhesive for repair.

Being organic in nature, *sanchipat* manuscripts are vulnerable to climatic conditions particularly to the moisture. The excess of relative humidity in the North-eastern states, where *sanchipat* was mostly used, put these manuscripts to further risk of fast decay. Preventive conservation of these manuscripts, particularly the protection from moisture, is therefore very relevant. The curative conservation, if required, should be undertaken with materials comparable with the original in strength and behaviour.

7

Preliminary Report on the Conservation of *Kaditas* (Black Manuscripts)

B. V. Kharbade

A *Kadita* or *Kadata* is a long piece of cloth covered with a thick paste, prepared out of ground tamarind seeds and charcoal powder, which appear like a thick black paper. It is folded in the form of book running into two to three hundred pages but opens like a roll. White soap stone pencil is used for writing on the *Kaditas.* Dr. A.K. Shastri[1] carried out detailed study on *Kaditas* of Shringeri Matha and classified them under two heads as *Nirūpas* (orders) and *Binnavattales* (letters of respect) and found that there are two hundred five and five hundred forty eight volumes belonging to the former and the latter category respectively. He mentioned that *Kaditas* contain original writings and other records that throw light on political, administrative, religious, economic and social conditions prevalent not only in Shringeri but also in different parts of Karnataka from fourteenth to nineteenth century, and his study establishes relation between the Shringeri Matha and the various secular powers like Vijayanagara, Kaladi, Marathas, the Wodiyars of Mysore, Hyder Ali, Tipu, the Nizam, chiefs of the various principalities and the British. *Kaditas* are mostly written in

Kannada but other languages like Sanskrit, Marathi, Tamil, Telugu and Persian have also been used.

The author of this report came to know about these unique manuscripts in the year 1988 when Dr. I.K. Bhatnagar, the then Project Officer of Regional Conservation Laboratory, sent some samples of *Kaditas* to the author at NRLC, Lucknow, for analysis to understand their composition. Fortunately, the author got the opportunity to work on *Kadita's* conservation as he took charge of this laboratory in 2002 and since then he has been trying to popularize the uniqueness of the *Kaditas* as well as the need for their conservation. This report is also an attempt in that direction.

Survey and State of Preservation

For surveying of *Kaditas*, a questionnaire was prepared and sent in August 2003 to about twenty public and private institutions including various religious Mathas in Karnataka but the response was very poor. According to the survey, most of the *Kaditas,* about eight hundred volumes, are in Sri Sri *Jagadguru* Shankaracharya Mahasamsthanam Dakshinamnaya, Sri Sharada Peetham, Shringeri, North Kanara District, Karnataka. The volumes have been catalogued and the catalogue formed a thesis for a Ph.D. Degree of theKarnataka University, which was published later as 'History of Shringerii'. *Kaditas* have been wrapped in two sheets of commercially available ply board securing properly with cotton rope as shown in Fig. 1, and then stacked on steel racks. This method of storing the *Kaditas* has been followed in all the institutions.

There is not much deterioration due to natural ageing of *Kaditas* but major cause of their decay is excessive humidity, which helps the growth of moulds, fungi and insects. Tunneling due to termite attack is quite common in most of the *Kaditas.* The microbes degrade the materials of the objects by secreting selective enzymes for their nutrients. Degradation of *Kaditas* due to moist condition could be explained through Fig. 2 to Fig. 4.

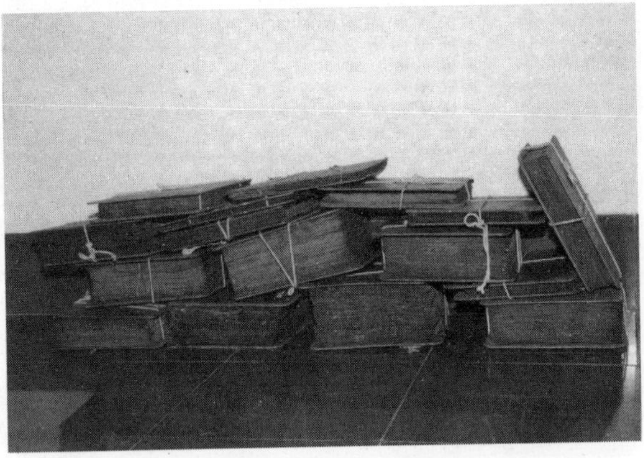

Fig 1: *Kaditas wrapped in between two sheets of commercially available ply board securing tightly with cotton rope.*

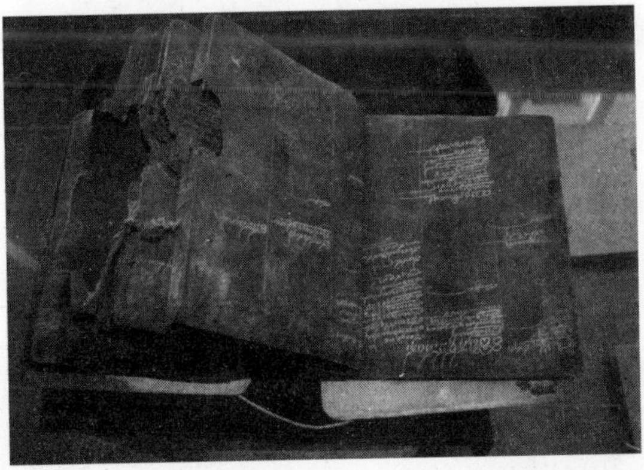

Fig. 2 : *Deterioration in Kaditas due to humid conditions, which facilitates the growth of moulds, fungi and insects (termite).*

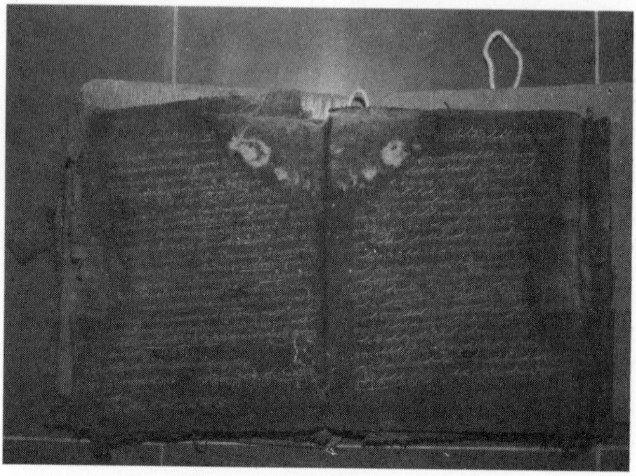

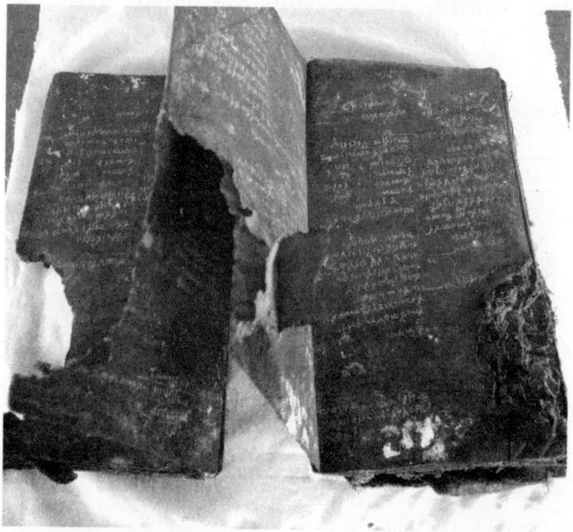

Fig. 3 and 4: *Deterioration in Kaditas due to humid conditions which facilitates the growth of moulds, fungi and insects (termite).*

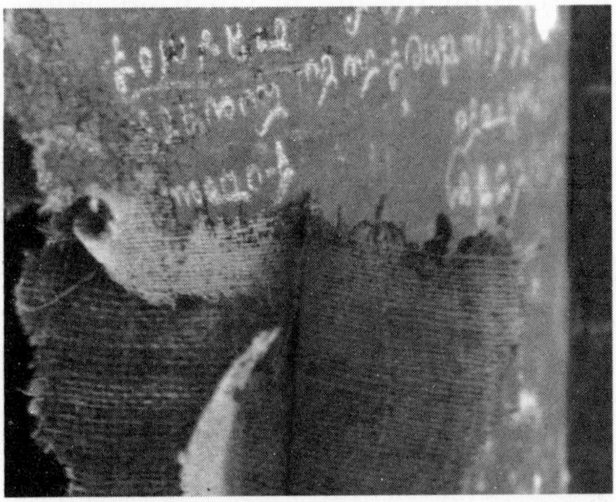

Fig. 5: *Show different layers of cloth used in making of Kaditas. The texture resembles to coarse handloom cloth.*

Case Studies

Scientific examination

This laboratory had received some *Kaditas* for the purpose of conservation treatment from Karnataka State Archives, Bangalore. On examining them, it was discovered that a few layers of the same or different cloth were used in making the *Kaditas.* The layers varied within the same object in order to get uniform and desired thickness. The paste of tamarind mixed with charcoal seemed to be applied on both sides of assembled layers of cloth. Fig. 5 shows separated layers of cloth in one of the samples. Simple burning test performed on the small yarn pulled out of the cloth confirmed the use of cotton cloth. Microscopic examination indicated that the texture of cloth was coarse and most probably the cloth used there was made on handloom as it appeared very similar to Khadi cloth which was prevalent in India during British period. Black paste on cloth tested positive for starch which may confirm the use of tamarind seed. Attempts were made to identify the paste using the standardized methods that confirmed the presence of polysaccharide group, but it could not ascertain the use of tamarind paste, whereas presence of charcoal in the paste was confirmed by microscopic examination. In order to identify the writing material, a small sample scrapped with fine-edged scalpel was subjected to micro-chemical tests to reassure its content of calcite, i.e. calcium carbonate, a common mineral of lime stone.

Conservation Problems and their Treatment

Kaditas received for conservation in this laboratory were heavily infested with mould and fungi. Although no living termite was found in the object, termite tunneling was quite visible in all the objects. Holes and loss of some areas are seen in some of the *Kaditas.* Some of the objects were more than two hundred years old but there was no occurence of brittleness, cracks and flaking in the black coating, which are quite obvious in a tamarind seed paste when mixed with charcoal. This needs a thorough research of the fact. Fungal growth and stains were moped gently with cotton buds soaked in rectified spirit. Then, the objects were cleaned with mixture of methyl alcohol and water (80:20). Holes were filled with freshly prepared paste of tamarind seed (procured from local market of Mysore) mixed with fine pure charcoal (obtained from chemical supplier) and 1% of orthophenyl phenol as a fungicide.

How to restore lost parts of the *Kaditas*? What materials should be used for that? Whether or not to use the same old materials? These are some of the questions which are being investigated in this laboratory.

Acknowledgements

The author is thankful to the authorities of the Karnataka State Archives, Bangalore for allowing him to work on their *Kaditas.* Thanks are also due to my colleagues Shri Minesh Hirenkhede and Shri Vithal Koneri for their help in preparing figures for this paper.

References

1. Shastry, A.K., "*Kaditas of Shringeri Matha in book,*" 2nd edition, *History of Shringeri,* Prasaranga, Karnataka University, Dharwad (1998), pp 53-56 .
2. Kharbade, B.V., Joshi, G.P., and Agrawal, O.P., "Effective thin layer chromatographic and hydrolysis method for the identification of plant gums of art objects," *Studies in Conservation,* New Delhi (1995), pp. 40-93.
3. Kharbade, B.V., "Use of reflectance techniques for infra red spectrophotometric analysis and examination of art objects," *Proceedings of the 18th International Symposium on the Conservation and Restoration of Cultural Property- Spectrometric Examination in Conservation,* October31- Nov.2, 1994 Tokyo, Japan, pp. 28-40.

8

Conservation of Manuscripts on Ivory

K.K. Gupta

The preservation of our cultural property is one of the major tasks of our times. Manuscripts are one form of the cultural property. Ancient man expressed himself by laboriously drawing pictures and symbols or writing on various different support materials.

Some early writing materials are—

Stone
Bricks
Wood
Leaves of tree, e.g. Palm leaf
Bark of tree, e.g. Birch bark
Parchment
Papyrus
Ivory

Ivory Manuscripts

In Imperial Rome ivory tablets that could be folded together and were covered with wax on the inside were used to write on. These were made by working a shallow depression into an ivory tablet leaving raised frame at the edges. Dark coloured molten wax consisting of beewax was generally used with admixture of oil, fats or resins, and fillers such as clay, charcoal and lamp black. Two or more such tablets of ivory were joined together with hinges, by rings or loops of wire or by leather or thread. From the end of fourth century AD, these diptychs (so called as they generally consist of two tablets) were decorated with figurative and ornamental relief carving on the outside. When the codex form of book appeared, these were reused as book covers.

In strict terms, true ivory comes from the tusks of elephants. This includes both African and Asian species and their prehistoric ancestor, the mammoth. Tusks and teeth from walrus, hippopotamus, boar and whales (sperm, killer and narwhal) are also commonly referred to as ivory, but some do not consider these to be true ivory. Generally speaking, however, ivory refers to the tusks or large teeth of these mammals. The age, sex, species and living conditions of the animal determine the properties of the ivory. The closer an ivory producing area is to the equator, the hotter, lower lying and more humid it is, the finer and more transparent is the ivory; the farther the area from the equator and the dryer it is, the coarser and denser the quality.

Processing of Ivory

Ivory is inherently a complex material and its composition and properties makes at very sensitive to water. Ivory is a mineralized collagenous matrix consisting mainly of calcium phosphate hydroxide $3Ca_3(PO_4)_2$ $Ca(OH)_2$. It has high moisture content when the tusk is first removed from the animal. This is then slowly dried in air and when the moisture falls to about 15%, it is worked by various methods such as:

- Carving
- Sawing
- Turning
- Engraving/etching
- Bending

- Grinding/polishing
- Colouring

Carving
Since ivory is harder and denser than wood, its carving is more of chipping and scrapping technique. Various types of chisels, files and scrappers are used for the purpose. Separate parts were usually put together by ivory dowels, with or without the use of animal glue.

Sawing
To make ivory slabs apt for writing or relief, narrow rectangles of ivory were sawed and then put together. This was done with sharp saws for otherwise there is a chance of its cracking.

Turning
Ivory is particularly suitable for turning because of its homogenous dense texture. Turned objects consisting of different parts are then screwed together.

Engraving/etching
Figurative drawing or text can be engraved into ivory and the incised lines are then blackened. Ivory can be covered with an etching ground; the lines are then incised in the ground and etched with acid. The nitric acid containing dissolved silver will produce black lines in addition to etching of ivory.

Bending
The ivory plaques can be bent after being softened in boiling water, if so required.

Grinding/polishing
After carving, sawing or etching, the plaques of ivory were smoothened by grinding and polishing. Slurry of fine pumice powder was among the abrasives used for grinding.

Colouring

Ivory has been used as such in its natural colour or by dying it with some dyes. Turmeric, cochineal, indigo, logwood and oak gall with verdigris are some of the dyes used in the past for colouring the ivory.

Deterioration

By the combined effect of the internal and external agencies of deterioration various types of damages are found in manuscripts on ivory

Deformation

Ivory is hygroscopic material and expands and contracts with changes in relative humidity. It expands in high relative humidity and contracts in dry conditions. Also since ivory is anisotropic in nature, the extent of expansion and contraction is different in different directions, resulting in cracking, warping and other distortions in fluctuating climatic conditions.

The stress created by the deformation due to changes in relative humidity, causes the joints of ivory to loose or the dowels used for joining them to break. The joints of the ivory covers of the books may also crack. The gold or silver leaf or ink used for writing may wrinkle if ivory contracts in dry conditions, while these may flake off by repeated expansion and contraction. Iron set in the ivory, such as dowels may cause the ivory to rupture because of the rusting of iron resulting in the increase in its volume.

Discolouration

The ivory material, because of being absorbent, has often been found discoloured through their contact with other materials. Rust spots from rusted iron, green discolouration from copper or its alloys, stains due to fungus in humid conditions are some such examples. Ivory may also acquire a patina because of age or excessive use or from the effects of smoke, dust, sweat, and sebaceous secretions. It becomes yellow in dark and stagnant conditions.

Salt Action

Bone or ivory from a salty environment will invariably absorb soluble salts, which will crystallize as the object dries. The action of salt crystallization causes physical strain resulting in flaking and cracking in ivory and can, in some cases, destroy the specimen.

Chemical changes

Ivory tends to get brittle in the course of time. The excavated ivory objects are altered by the continued action of water, which decomposes oscine, the organic matter of ivory, changing it into a spongy substance. It may also get encrusted by deposits of lime, silica and other minerals under these conditions, hardening it like a fossil.

Conservation

Preventive Conservation

- To control temperature and relative humidity between 20-25°C and 45-55% respectively, without sharp fluctuations even between these limits.
- Strong temporary heating, such as that from direct sunlight or spotlight should be avoided.
- Protect them from contact with coloured and dyed materials.
- Should be wrapped in white acid-free tissue paper while in storage.

Curative Conservation

Ivory is a complex material and its composition and properties eliminate many forms of treatment from the start. However, there are three main operations in the conservation of ivory material. These are:

- Cleaning
- Straightening
- Re-inforcement

Cleaning Methods

Ivory can be cleaned with a soft brush and mixture of water and alcohol. Alcohol helps better penetration of water and also makes the mixture fast-drying. Prolonged contact with water may lead to the warping of ivory. Because of hygroscopic and anisotropic property, ivory should always be evenly moistened from all the sides. The cleaning should be as quick as possible and with as little water as possible. Drying of ivory, however, should not be accelerated by heating.

Erasers can also be used for cleaning of ivory manuscripts. Powdered eraser can be gently rubbed on ivory, using either the soft brush or the fingertip (wearing white cotton gloves, so that the ivory does not absorb the oils, etc. from the hands). One must choose the softer eraser such as vinyl eraser, particularly in case of weak and fragile object, and gently brush away all of the eraser flakes after cleaning. Cleaning should always be started with the gentlest of the methods, gradually moving to harsher techniques, as required. Care should, however, be taken that the treatment does not produce abrasion marks.

Removal of soluble salts

The soluble salts present in the ivory objects must be removed in order to make the object stable. Different methods are used depending upon the condition of the object.

1. If the bone/ivory is structurally sound, the salts can be diffused by rinsing in successive baths of alcohol containing about 20% of water. The process is repeated until all the soluble salt are removed. In order to determine the level of salts in the rinse water,

it is necessary to use a conductivity meter. One can alternatively use the silver nitrate test to detect the presence of sodium chloride. When sodium chlorides are no longer present, it is reasonable to assume that the bulk of the soluble salts have been removed.

2. If the ivory is structurally unsound, it can be consolidated with a 2% solution of Paraloid B-72 and then rinsed. The soluble salts will be diffused through the resin, albeit much more slowly, during the rinsing treatment.

Ivory should be dried as fast as possible after the wet treatment mentioned above. It is dried by passing through a series of alcohol baths (80 percent alcohol/20 percent water), increasing the alcohol content of the baths to 90 percent, and a final bath of 100 percent alcohol). The object can then be taken through two baths of acetone. In some cases, when the materials is fragile, it is advisable to take the object through at least two baths of diethyl ether. In most cases, after the object has been taken through two baths of acetone, it is reasonable to assume that all the water has been removed.

Removal of stains

If it is necessary to remove stains from ivory, some means of mechanical removal using picks or other tools are always recommended over any chemical treatment. While using chemicals always make sure that the area is wet with water before any chemical is applied. This ensures that the treating chemical remains on the surface of the artefact and is not absorbed into the object. One must also be very careful not to remove any original surface coats, ink, paint or patina during the process.

Iron stains

It is suggested that 5-10% oxalic acid can be used to remove the iron stains from ivory. For stubborn stains, 5% ammonium citrate can be used alone or if necessary can be or followed by 5% oxalic acid.

Sulfide stains

The removal of sulfide stains is possible by the use of mild bleaching agent such as 5-10% of hydrogen peroxide. Stained ivory may be placed in a hydrosulfite solution followed by dilute hydrogen peroxide to remove any remaining stain. Weak and fragile ivory should be treated with localized applications of the solution with a brush or swab. If such ivory pieces are submerged, the evolution of carbon dioxide from the decomposition of the $CaCO_3$ may break up the object. Very fragile ivory may be treated by the application of the chemicals only locally to stubborn spots, which is followed by the application of water and blotting it.

After the removal of stains, it is necessary to rinse the artifact in mixture of alcohol and water to remove all residue of the treating chemical, followed by drying in alcohol baths, and water then consolidate with a resin, if required.

Re-inforcement

Weak and fragile ivory sheets can be consolidated by introducing some suitable resin into it. Any resin solution used for the purpose, must be diluted to decrease the viscosity and increase its ability to penetrate into the sheets being treated. A 5-10% solution of a suitable transparent synthetic resin such as Paraloid B-72 may be used.

For surface consolidation, resin solution may be applied with a brush. It is preferable to use dilute solution, allowing it to dry, and then applying a second coat, if required. This procedure should be repeated several times in order to allow for sufficient resin to be absorbed by the material and there by re-inforcing it. Complete immersion of the artifact in the consolidating resin gives excellent results where the whole thickness of the sheet requires consolidation. The complete immersion in the resin under vacuum is considered to be the best method for consolidating most ivory artefacts.

In case the ivory sheet has holes and gaps, it can be structurally consolidated and restored by impregnation with mixture of wax and resin in the ratio of 3:1. The gaps and hollows can also be filled with this material mixed with suitable pigment to give it the right shade. Cracks in the ivory, as a rule, should not be filled. If at all, hard filler should never be used for filling as it causes strain on the original ivory due to the fluctuations in the atmospheric condition, and may produce more cracks. Wax resin mixture to which some pigment is added to match colour, can sometimes be used for filling the cracks, as this has some flexibility. Missing parts, in otherwise strong ivory sheets, can be replaced with ivory pieces of suitable size. Care, however, should be taken that the direction of the fibres is similar to the original and is not too strong as compared to the original.

At times the re-inforcement of ivory sheets is achieved by giving an additional support. In such cases some additional factors must be taken into account for selecting the supporting material. The material must be flexible enough to follow extreme changes in the ivory's contours and the adhesive must be strong enough to adhere firmly to the surface and yet flexible enough to allow the movement of ivory with changes in environmental condtions. A material which initially adheres may eventually peel or shear away since ivory surfaces are often polished. Adhesive used however, should not be too strong, for otherwise strain caused by it may lead to cracks in the ivory sheets.

Lately, several materials are being considered for reinforcing the cracked ivory. Adhesives containing solvents which might leach the constituents of the ivory, or any material requiring such a solvent for its removal, should not be used. As a rule the adhesive used should be slightly weaker than the object itself, so that in case of strain, the restoration may give way rather than causing a new break.

Ivory, being organic and anisotropic in character, is very much vulnerable to deterioration such as cracking and deformation due to fluctuations in RH. So keeping ivory manuscripts in controlled and stable environmental conditions is the first priority in order to save them. The material used for the curative conservation of ivory manuscripts should not put any physical strain on these. Prolonged exposure to water during their conservation must also be avoided.

9

Studies on Methods of Lamination of Birch Bark Manuscripts

D.G. Suryawanshi

With time and due to aging, birch bark sheets become fragile and brittle. In order to strengthen them, it is necessary to give them an additional support. If the writing is only on one side, the support can be given from the back. However, since the manuscripts are normally written on both sides, relining with an opaque material is not desirble instead lamination of the folios between two transparent sheets is a possibility.

In order to do that, a supporting material and an adhesive is needed. In the case of paper, lamination materials like cellulose acetate foils and Japanese tissue paper or thin polythene are being universally used. For birch bark also, being similar to paper, these materials have been used but it was observed that they are not as effective as on paper materials. The author, therefore, decided to test combinations of different adhesives and supporting materials for imparting strength to birch bark sheets. These studies were conducted to ascertain their feasibility, as well as their properties in relation to the birch bark.

Adhesives

(1) Carboxy Methyl Cellulose (CMC)

(2) Methyl Cellulose (MC)
(3) Maida (Fine Wheat Flour)
(4) Dextrine
(5) A mixture of CMC and Maida (1:2)
(6) A mixture of CMC and Dextrine (1:2)

Supporting Materials
(1) Nepalese hand made paper
(2) Japanese tissue paper
(3) Indian tissue paper
(4) Chiffon
(5) Chiffon and Indian tissue paper
(6) Chiffon and Japanese tissue paper
(7) Nepalese and Indian tissue paper

Experimental

The solutions of the above adhesives were prepared in the concentration of 1.0, 1.5, and 2.0 percentages each in distilled water.

The supporting materials to be used for laminating the documents were prepared in a specific size of 24 × 16 cms. approximately. The adhesive solutions were applied on supporting materials which were kept on a thin polythene sheet on a smooth table. Fine sable hair brushes were used to apply the solutions over two sheets of the supporting material. The document was then sandwiched between the sheets of supporting material. The assembly was left overnight for drying at room temperature. Prepared standard sample specimens were tested physically (Folding endurance) and optically (Brightness percentages) according to the standard methods of TAPPI and ASIM.

The samples were aged artificially by keeping them in an oven at 105 ± 2°C temperature for 24, 48 and 72 hours duration. Every time the brightness and folding endurance

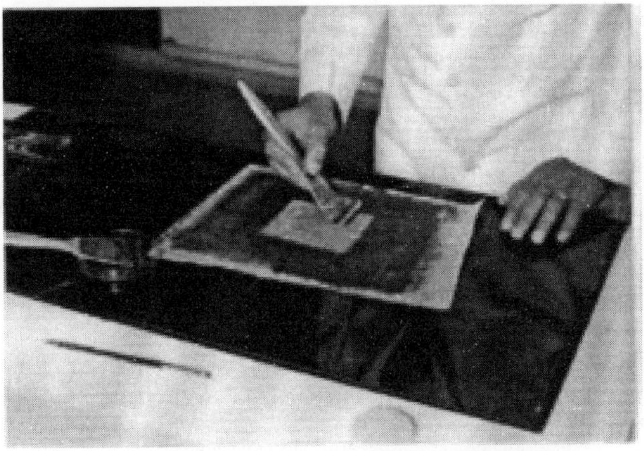

Fig. 1: *Laminating a birch bark sample in between two layers of Japanese tissue paper by using CMC paste.*

were measured. The brightness was measured on Gloss/ Reflectance meter (AIM-66) manufactured by M/s. AIMIL, New Delhi (India). The folding strength was measured on the Folding Endurance Tester, Model Kohler Molin M/s. Lorentzen and Wetter, Stockholm (Sweden).

Measurement of folding endurance of supporting materials which were pasted with Carboxy Methyl Cellulose (CMC) in different concentrations before and after artificial aging.

Supporting Materials	Before aging			Folding Endurance at 0.5 Kg. tension After artificials aging, hours. 24			48			72		
	1.0	1.5	2.0	1.0	1.5	2.0	1.0	1.5	2.0	1.0	1.5	2.0
Nepalese Tissue Paper	1432	1416	1500	1402	1398	1427	1389	1322	1368	1088	908	768
Japanese Tissue Paper	442	448	406	404	396	322	365	280	273	263	216	212
Indian Tissue Paper	906	932	922	900	916	908	872	847	843	692	639	462

Results and Discussions:

On observing the results of folding endurance and brightness, it is seen that all adhesives have their individual characteristics, inspite of having the same property of stickiness. Some of them have shown good results on supporting materials, whereas other have poor performance.

Measurement of folding endurance of supporting materials which were pasted with Methyl Cellulose in different concentration before and after artificial aging.

Folding Endurance at 0.5 Kg. tension

Materials	Before aging			After artificials aging, hours.								
				24		48	72					
	1.0	1.5	2.0	1.0	1.5	2.0	1.0	1.5	2.0	1.0	1.5	2.0
Nepalese Tissue Paper	1054	1056	1052	1024	1010	1020	850	895	828	624	630	604
Japanese Tissue Paper	625	628	626	498	489	479	470	464	448	280	288	260
Indian Tissue Paper	895	907	888	892	890	872	735	746	716	681	700	695

Measurement of folding endurance of supporting materials which were pasted with Maida (wheat flour) in different concentration, before and after artificial ageing.

Folding Endurance at 0.5 Kg. tension

Materials	Before aging			After artificials aging, hours.								
				24		48	72					
	1.0	1.5	2.0	1.0	1.5	2.0	1.0	1.5	2.0	1.0	1.5	2.0
Nepalese Tissue Paper	1038	1028	1022	1018	948	962	935	916	939	512	527	517
Japanese Tissue Paper	436	448	410	433	436	401	462	337	299	285	278	208
Indiam Tissue Paper	952	969	948	950	948	942	910	882	903	872	845	834

Measurement of folding endurance of supporting materials which were pasted with the mixture of CMC and Maida flour (1:2) in different concentrations before and after artificial aging.

Folding Endurance at 0.5 Kg. tension

Materials	Before aging			After artificials aging, hours.								
				24			48			72		
	1.0	1.5	2.0	1.0	1.5	2.0	1.0	1.5	2.0	1.0	1.5	2.0
Nepalese Tissue Paper	1102	1098	1097	1075	1077	1088	988	962	978	902	900	908
Japanese Tissue Paper	522	499	498	485	490	482	423	431	411	378	382	373
Indian Tissue Paper	950	941	952	926	920	921	889	872	844	790	783	776

Measurement of folding endurance of supporting materials which applied with the mixture of CMC and Dextrin (1:2) in different concentrations before and after artificial aging.

Folding Endurance at 0.5 Kg. tension

Materials	Before aging			After artificials aging, hours.								
				24			48			72		
	1.0	1.5	2.0	1.0	1.5	2.0	1.0	1.5	2.0	1.0	1.5	2.0
Nepalese Tissue Paper	833	839	802	820	803	795	732	699	685	508	518	510
Japanese Tissue Paper	418	410	414	412	390	397	381	347	356	303	298	304
Indian Tissue Paper	736	715	742	685	672	685	601	621	610	554	505	518

The Chemicals Carboxy Methyl Cellulose and Methyl Cellulose (Glutofix-600) are found to be similar in nature.

Both of them are having high degree of adhesive chracteristic. The supporting materials pasted with these chemicals have shown good strength towards folding endurance and high degree of brightness. Even after artificial aging the folding strength is good as well as the change in appearance is very little as compared to the rest of the adhesives.

On application over Nepalese hand made paper it is seen that at 2% solution of CMC and MC the original brightness 56% is increased by 69% whereas the folding endurance capacity was found to be very satisfactory even after aging for 72 hours.

In comparison to CMC and MC, maida paste and dextrin were found to be inferior in adhesive property. However, adding of these materials, the brightness could be increased and the folding strength of supporting material were also found satisfactory. On the other hand, maida paste is found better than dextrin as it is having good sticking property at 2% concentration.

On testing of brightness and folding endurance of supporting materials, there is no sppreciable change observed in respect of variable concentration of adhesives.

Original brightness of supporting materials increases with the application of adhesives. The brightness of supporting materials applied with starch or maida and dextrin is found to be comparatively more than rest of the adhesives. It may be due to their original brightness; however, the sticking property is poor.

Study of the mixture of CMC and starch and CMC with Dextrine in ratio 1:2, indicates that the brightness and folding endurance results are more appropriate and their folding endurance did not drop on aging.

The brightness of Japanese Tissue (94) and Chiffon (87) is excellent and on application of adhesives, it further increased. Therefore, even after aging for seventy-two hours the colour did not change significantly.

The folding strength of chiffon was found to be more than 5000 before and after its aging, whereas in the case of Japanese and Indian tissue paper the strength was observed to be less after aging. In all the cases, it was seen that as the concentration increased, the folding strength and brightness both decreased. The former may be due to the increasing stiffness and later due to greater thickness of supporting materials.

All the supporting materials are useful but they can be used according to the state of the object. If the documents are very fragile the supporting material may be hand made paper or chiffon. In the case of birch bark, fading of ink is a common problem and on lamination with chiffon or Nepalese paper the writing will get somewhat obscured. The mixed study of two supporting materials, therefore, has been done to solve the problems of transparency of letters.

Measurement of brightness of supporting materials by using CMC in different concentration before and after atificial aging.

Materials	Before aging			After artificials aging, hours.								
				24			48			72		
	1.0	1.5	2.0	1.0	1.5	2.0	1.0	1.5	2.0	1.0	1.5	2.0
Nepalese Tissue Paper	67	68	67	62	60	63	60	63	59	61	58	56
Japanese Tissue Paper	96	96	97	96	95	96	95	95	95	94	92	92
Chiffon	90	91	90	89	90	89	88	89	87	87	87	87
Chiffon & Indian Tissue	78	79	78	78	78	75	77	77	75	74	73	73
Chiffon & Japanese Tissue	89	90	89	89	90	88	86	87	87	85	85	85

Measurement of brightness of supporting materials which sere pasted with Methyl Cellulose in different concentrations before and after aging.

Materials	Before aging			After artificials aging, hours. 24			48			72		
	1.0	1.5	2.0	1.0	1.5	2.0	1.0	1.5	2.0	1.0	1.5	2.0
Nepalese Tissue Paper	66	67	68	67	67	65	62	60	60	61	61	59
Japanese Tissue Paper	97	97	97	98	96	97	96	95	95	85	82	87
Chiffon	90	90	91	91	91	90	89	89	89	88	87	87
Chiffon& Ind. tissue	79	76	77	79	77	77	78	77	76	77	74	73
Chiffon & Jap. tissue	89	89	89	89	90	90	88	88	89	87	88	89

Measurement of brightness of supporting materials which were pasted with starch and Maida paste in different percentages and after artificial aging.

Materials	Before aging			After artificials aging, hours. 24			48			72		
	1.0	1.5	2.0	1.0	1.5	2.0	1.0	1.5	2.0	1.0	1.5	2.0
Nepalese Tissue Paper	76	75	76	76	76	75	74	74	73	72	71	71
Japanese Tissue Paper	98	98	97	95	96	96	92	90	92	89	88	88
India Tissue Paper	91	92	91	90	90	89	88	88	89	82	84	84
Chiffon	89	91	89	90	91	91	89	88	87	87	87	87
Chiffon & Ind. tissue	79	79	82	79	79	79	78	78	78	74	74	74
Chiffon & Jap. tissue	89	90	91	90	90	90	89	89	87	84	83	83

Measurement of Brightness of supporting materials which were pasted with the mixture of CMC and Starch (1:2) in various concentriation and tested before and after artificial aging.

Materials	Before aging			After artificials aging, hours. 24			48			72		
	1.0	1.5	2.0	1.0	1.5	2.0	1.0	1.5	2.0	1.0	1.5	2.0
Nepalese Tissue Paper	76	75	76	76	75	75	75	74	74	71	71	69
Japanese Tissue Paper	87	88	89	87	88	88	86	85	86	83	82	82
India tis. paper	89	88	89	88	89	89	86	86	87	86	85	85
Chiffon	90	89	90	90	88	88	86	85	85	83	83	81
Chiffon & Ind. tissue	78	80	77	78	80	76	76	76	74	72	71	70
Chiffon & Japanese tissue	88	88	89	88	89	88	84	83	84	81	81	80

Measurement of brightness of supporting materials which applied with the mixture of CMC and Dextrine (1:2) in different concentrations and tested before and after artificial aging.

Materials	Before aging			After artificials aging, hours. 24			48			72		
	1.0	1.5	2.0	1.0	1.5	2.0	1.0	1.5	2.0	1.0	1.5	2.0
Nepalese Tissue Paper	68	68	68	68	67	67	66	67	67	66	67	66
Japanese Tissue Paper	96	97	97	92	92	93	92	91	92	87	87	88
Indian tissue paper	90	89	89	91	90	89	88	85	85	83	83	82

Chiffon	89	88	88	88	88	88	88	87	87	86	86	85
Chiffon & Indian Tissue	89	88	88	89	88	88	88	86	86	82	81	81
Chiffon and Japanese tissue	88	89	89	89	89	89	87	86	86	81	80	80

On the basis of the results of folding endurances and brightness, following conclusions were drawn.

In order to laminate the bark objects, chiffon and Indian tissue as well as Japanese tissue were found suitable for use to develop the strength. CMC and MC were found very good adhesives to refix the separated layers of birch bark and for lamination as well.

Cellulose acetate film and polythene sheets were not found satisfactory because of the non-fibrous material and of poor binding property. Carboxy Methyl Cellulose, Methyl Cellulose and their mixtures with maida paste at lower consistency can be used for lamination.

10

Conservation of Manuscripts on Parchment

K.K. Gupta

Before the introduction of paper, ancient people used stone, copper plate, palm leaf, birch bark *(Bhuja patra)*, cloth fabric, *jute* pulp paper and parchment as writing materials. Throughout the entire middle ages, parchment, along with papyrus, was the predominant writing material in Europe and in the Middle East. Only with the invention of paper and the dissemination of bookmaking did this highly efficient and effective product disappear from general use.

Parchment is the dehaired, untanned skin of various animals such as calves, sheep and goats dried under tension on frames. A distinction is occasionally made between vellum, made from calf skins, and parchment, from all other skins; but the words have often been used interchangably. Although parchment has largely been replaced by paper, it still finds an important place as writing material for some permanent and quality documents, such as contracts, maps, plans, family trees etc. In India, being considered impure, parchment was not much used for writing, particularly for sacred inscriptions. In west, the thin, fine textured parchment was preferred for manuscripts and miniature paintings, whereas thicker coarser grade was used for book bindings. The copies of acts of British Parliament signed by the queen are on vellum.

Parchment achieved importance as writing material because of:

- Its lightness and flexibility
- More suitable for ink and colours
- Can be written on both the sides
- Possibility of erasing and correction
- Light in colour, so create contrast with ink and so easy to read
- Stitching possible, and so possibility of codex binding, which was not there in palm leaf or papyrus etc.
- High tearing strength
- Long term stability and so suitable for permanent records
- Re-usable.

History of parchment manufacture

The word 'parchment' derived its name from the name of the ancient city Pergamon. According to the reports of various classical authors, parchment was 'invented' by Eumenes of Pergamon (197—159 BC). The development of the codex, i.e. text bound in book form, from the fourth century onward gradually replaced the scrolls, which were used mostly for deeds and similar official documents. The introduction of parchment codices, whose structure and binding resemble that of today's books, brought many advantages, including that the bound pages are simpler to handle than scrolls.

The biochemical structure of parchment

The essential components of parchment from animal skins are the fibers of the skin tissue. This extra cellular matrix in the skin is composed of bundles of long-chained fibrils of the high molecular weight proteins—collagen and elastin. In living skin, the intercellular spaces are filled with fluid or plasma.

The production of parchment

The preparation of parchment for the purpose of writing showed very little change over the years. The skin of many animals was used for making of parchment. The most common among these were sheep, calf and goat skin. The age and colour of the animal determine the quality of parchment. The younger the animal, the finer as a rule the parchment made out of it. Fine grade of parchment made from calf skin is known as vellum. The first step for making parchment involves immersing the fresh animal skin for two to six weeks in a 5—10% solution of slaked lime (process is known as liming). The different layers of the skin swell at different rates and gradually begin to break up. The epidermis reacts most quickly. Because the hairs have their roots here, after the immersion process, the hairs along with their roots are easily removed by shaving with a crescent-shaped knife. The skin is then reversed and the remains of fat and muscles are likewise removed from the flesh side. After washing, the transparent skin is stretched and dried on a frame. These physical processes orient the fibers in sheets and open up the inner structure of the collagen so that air penetrates between the layers causing the parchment to become opaque, and thus making it suitable for writing or for decoration on both sides.

To enhance the surface properties for writing, both sides of the dried parchment are carefully polished so that they are neither too rough nor too smooth. Polishing (also known as pouncing) is done while the skin is still in stretched condition on the frame, either with a crescent-shaped knife, with pumice or with specially prepared sanding bread. For the latter, bread dough is mixed with glass splinters, formed into small rolls and baked. For more sensitivity of the parchment surface it is treated with such prepared sanding bread rather than with pumice or a knife. With slight carelessness in the use of knife, the skin can be damaged quite quickly; pumices are not completely homogenous and contain hard stone nodules, which may cause scratches on the parchment surface. Cuts and tears that occur before the stretching procedure are usually sewn before the skin is put into the frame, so that they don't stretch or expand during drying. They can be cut out after drying, but often they are left in the parchment and can be noticed in the old manuscripts.

The Deterioration of Parchment Manuscripts

The parchment manuscripts are quite durable as compared to other organic writing materials commonly used. However, inappropriate humidity and temperature are main deteriorating factors for parchment manuscripts.

Relative Humidity

The main factor of deterioration of parchment is humidity. The parchment is hygroscopic in nature. On prolonged exposure to moisture, the collagen, which is its main constituent undergoes degradation through hydrolysis along with the degradation of binding medium in the illustrations. Prolonged exposure to relative humidity over 65% cause gradual decomposition of proteins and favours the growth of micro-organisms. The collagen is further degraded by the growth of micro-organisms, making the parchment thinner and fluffy. Parchment cockles in high relative humidity. If books on parchment are exposed to high humidity the edges of the pages take up the moisture and cockle. The paint layer and the parchment support expand and contract differently due to the changes in relative humidity, which results in their relative movement, ultimately leading to cleavage and flaking of the paint

Parchment partially gets converted into glue on

prolonged contact with water, which may lead to sticking of the folios because of their own weight or of the weight of overlying manuscripts. In dry environment, below 40% relative humidity, the parchment hardens and becomes brittle. At higher relative humidity it may regain its flexibility, but prolonged dry conditions may cause irreversible damage.

High humidity or excessive water also encourages molds to grow or causes the parchment to become transparent and to decompose.

Heat

Parchment is much more sensitive to heat than paper and its sensitivity depends upon its age. New parchment can be irreversibly damaged by the temperature over sixty degree. The old parchment, on the other hand, may irreversibly shrink and become brittle even at forty degree.

Light

Parchment is less sensitive to light than paper, though the painting and writing on it may be damaged in a similar way as in the case of paper paintings. If the parchment is strongly illuminated, the heat may act as an additional source of damage.

Reaction to acids

There is not much problem of acidity in parchment because of the treatment with lime during the process of its making. Inks and paints that release acids such as iron gall ink and verdigris, however, can eat away the parchment as in case of paper if exposed to moisture for a prolonged period. The lime residues also give certain protection against microorganisms which prefer slightly acidic nutrient substrates. But the residual lime present in it may weaken the bonds between parchment and paint or ink.

Conservation

Conservation can be classified into Preventive Conservation and Curative Conservation.

Preventive Conservation:

Preventive conservation is the control of all the deteriorating factors. It has the advantage of taking care of the whole collection simultaneously, without any actual interaction with each of them. It the environment is controlled in a proper way, the damaging effect on the whole collection is significantly reduced.

The preventive conservation of parchment involves control of temperature between 20°C and 25°C and relative humidity between 45% and 55% without sharp fluctuation even between these limits. The parchment manuscripts should also be protected from direct sunlight

Sheets of parchment should be kept in shallow drawers made of wood or non corroding metals. Some hygroscopic material such as acid-free paper or cotton cloth should be stored along with parchment in order to buffer the humidity to some extent

Curative Conservation

Curative conservation refers to undoing the damage the parchment manuscripts have undergone, and to bring them back, as close as possible, to its original condition. It mainly involves their cleaning and reinforcement. There is no general solution for the conservation of parchment manuscripts. The conservation operations and their sequence depend upon the condition of the manuscripts.

Opening

One of the problems encountered in parchment restoration are folds and wrinkles, which may be there for ages in some documents. Creases in manuscripts gradually weaken them at these areas. If the parchment sheet is rolled or folded and is very stiff, the first thing to be done is to open and straighten it after giving it some moisture. The correct amount of moisture is transferred by wrapping it in damp cloth followed by application of pressure to unfold it. The pressure is applied gradually after the parchment has become sufficiently pliable. Too much of pressure may break it while too prolonged exposure to moisture may make it sticky. The time of exposure depends upon the thickness of the sheet and the extent of its tanning, if present. If moisture alone fails to give required results, the sheet has to be swabbed locally with weak acetic acid and the process mentioned above be repeated. While doing so, it must be kept in mind that unrolled or unfolded sheets are allowed to dry under tension to avoid any risk of waviness.

Cleaning

Cleaning is an important as well as risky operation. The aims of cleaning can be twofold—one is to enable a better reading of the text which might be covered by surface dirt (though this is not always a wise decision to choose cleaning since better readability also be sometimes achieved through non-contact methods such as photography), the other aim is the aesthetic aspect, which can be considered of less importance for valuable documents where the long-term maintenance of a stable condition has a higher priority than the aesthetic appearance. Since cleaning is an irreversible operation, it is very important to identify as to what exactly is to be cleaned, before starting the process of cleaning.

Traditional surface cleaning of parchment is based on methods adapted from paper conservation and includes dry as well as wet cleaning. However, unlike paper, parchment should not be immersed in water or be washed with it. The cleaning of parchment is usually restricted to dry surface cleaning. Dry cleaning of parchment is carried out with different kinds of erasers, depending on the surface structure of the parchment, the state of preservation and the adhesion of the ink to the parchment surface. A variety of commercially available erasers are used and most of them are based on plasticized polyvinyl chloride. However, the mechanical treatment of the parchment surface may cause considerable damage to the fibre structure. In addition, fragments of ink may get dislodged and ingrained on the surface. Dry cleaning methods, therefore, are usually avoided if the parchment is in an advanced state of deterioration or the adhesion of the ink to the surface is poor.

Wet cleaning methods include, among others, the use of saliva, industrial methylated spirit (pure or mixed with water), and ethanol (96 % v/v) with water, and accumulations are removed machanically. The mixture is applied with cotton wool swabs and causes less mechanical pressure than the use of erasers. This may, however, cause damages such as loss of opacity or a change from a smooth to a rougher surface. Another major problem related to water-based treatments of parchment is that a visually intact fibre structure can be transformed into a gelatinous substance in contact with water. Carbon ink used on manuscripts may be affected by water treatment, while the corrosion of iron gall ink may lead to some irreversible changes such as fading or yellowing. Water treatment of parchment, therefore should be as fast as possible.

Removal of local stains from manuscripts is sometimes considered important for aesthetic reason. The methods and materials for their removal depend upon their type. Fat stains, for example, can be removed by sprinkling talc or quick lime over the stain and then shaking them off the next day. The use of acetone or isopropyl alcohol for removal of these stains proves to be more useful in most of the cases. Water stains on parchment can be removed or reduced by the application of water in mixture with isopropyl alcohol.

Acidity is generally not a problem in case of parchment manuscripts, because of the processing of skin with lime during the preparation of parchment. In case acidity is present, parchment can be deacidified by swabbing with pads of isopropyl alcohol containing lime water or pads of 5% aqueous solution of salts such as sodium borate or lactate, and finally swabbing it with water. In case of presence of water sensitive ink, it is important to fix it before any aqueous treatment by temporary application of 1 % solution of paraloid B72 in toluene or cellulose acetate in acetone.

Consolidation

The aim of any consolidation treatment is to arrest the flaking or powdering of paint or ink from the surface. Since the main cause of powdering and flaking is the degradation or loss of binding media in these, consolidation involves the introduction of some suitable binder (consolidant) within the paint/ink or between the paint/ink and the surface of parchment respectively, as the case may be.

The adhesive bond between two surfaces can be durable only if the binder and the surfaces to be adhered are compatible to each other. The consolidant, therefore, should be compatible with both the media and the support. It should also not create any visual change in the area while being treated, and should have good ageing characteristics. In addition, the technique for applying the consolidant should be controllable so that the surrounding media is not disturbed and no consolidant is deposited on the existing paint or ink.

One of the consolidation methods is to employ a very dilute (approximately 1 %) solution of leaf gelatin that is kept warm. Since it is obtained from animals, gelatin has the advantage of having the behaviour similar to parchment. The adhesive is absorbed into the cracks and losses more successfully if a small amount of ethanol is applied first to the area being treated. Ethanol can also be added directly to the adhesive in the bottle in order to further reduce the surface tension of the consolidant and thereby increasing its penetration. Since the water gradually evaporates out of the warm solution of gelatin over a few hours, one must regularly check the viscosity of the adhesive and add more water, if necessary, in order to keep it at the desired concentration. Ultrasonic Mister has been found to be very useful for the treatment of crumbly or brittle paint that are often disturbed by liquid consolidants.

Repair

Before any repair is undertaken, it is important that the parchment is relaxed. This can be done by controlled humidification. In large folio-sized manuscript codices, and in others that have especially thin parchment leaves, creases are developed on the pages as the books are repeatedly opened and during their use. To relax and then flatten out these sharp creases and folds, the parchment must be humidified in a controlled manner, preferably without affecting the surrounding undamaged areas.

Material for the repair of parchment manuscripts is chosen on the basis of its strength, flexibility, thickness and opacity, which should be comparable with that of original parchment. The best material for this is gold beater's parchment. Japanese tissue paper and silk gauge can also be used for the repair of holes and tears. Glue can be used as adhesive for the repair. Honey, gum Arabic, egg white and flour paste can be added to glue to control its strength, viscosity and flexibility.

Many new techniques for the repair of parchment manuscripts have also been developed. These are either the use of adhesive-coated tissues and animal membranes for the repair of splits and tears, or the pulp-filling of losses in parchment manuscripts and documents. The new adhesive-coated tissues and transparent membranes have proved to be especially useful for the repair of extremely deteriorated mold-damaged parchment that is adversely affected by liquid adhesives and is too weak to support a mend made with new parchment or heavier types of paper. These materials have often been prepared using Japanese tissue and goldbeater's skin and adhesives such as methyl cellulose, hydroxy propyl cellulose or Klucel, mixture of acrylic resins and isinglass.

Parchment, being organic in nature and very sensitive to moisture, is very much vulnerable to deterioration. The writing on it contains ink and pigments, which have altogether different properties and hence make them more prone to decay. It is, therefore, very important to keep them in controlled environment for their long-term preservation. The materials for its curative conservation should also have properties similar to those of parchment.

11

Storage of Manuscripts and Conservation Guidelines

V. Jeyaraj

There is a natural tendency to relax conservation vigilance when the museum objects are out of sight in storage or in vaults. The basic principle of storage is to keep the objects in a physically secured environment and yet to permit ready access for inspection, before their removal to the galleries, storage or other locations. One must remember that the storage infrastructure plays a very important role in the preservation of manuscripts. The building as well as the furniture for the purpose of storage, methods, techniques, and other facilities related to it, and proper coordination between the collection keepers/curators and the chemists are key factors for the upkeep of the manuscripts.

Storage Devices

There are various storage devices that are expected to meet the physical and environmental criteria intended for preserving the museum objects, especially metallic objects, against damages.

Stacking

Paintings and flat framed works, copper plate grants, etc.,

may be placed on pads and stacked vertically using cardboard as separators. In case of group-stacking, it is necessary to ensure that the pads are skid-proof, that the angle of stacking is average, and that the largest objects are kept first. Three-dimensional objects, like bronze icons, vessels and other large objects should be, placed on pallets to permit easy handling and lifting.

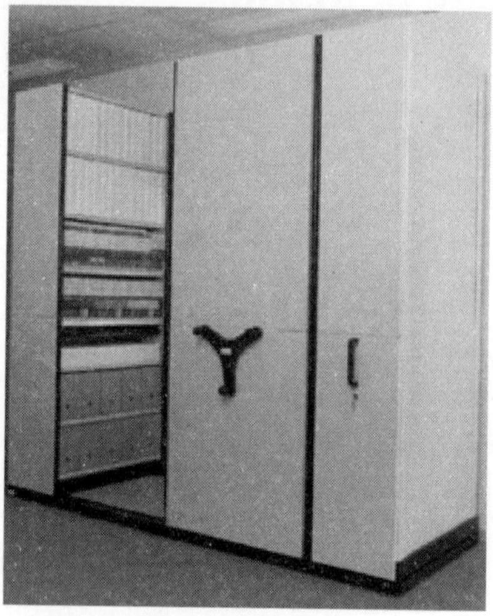

Shelving

Shelves may be constructed either of wood or preferably of metal for storage of two-dimensional or three-dimensional metallic objects. Vertical slots may be designed for flat items, such as manuscripts and bays are set up for objects. Boxes of different sizes may be made and objects are kept in these, wrapped with acid-free tissue paper. This method will utilize all the spaces available in the shelves.

Drawers and Cabinets

Drawers are used for flat objects like copper plate grants, large tokens and also, when appropriately designed, for small metallic objects. Interleaves of acid-free tissue paper are used

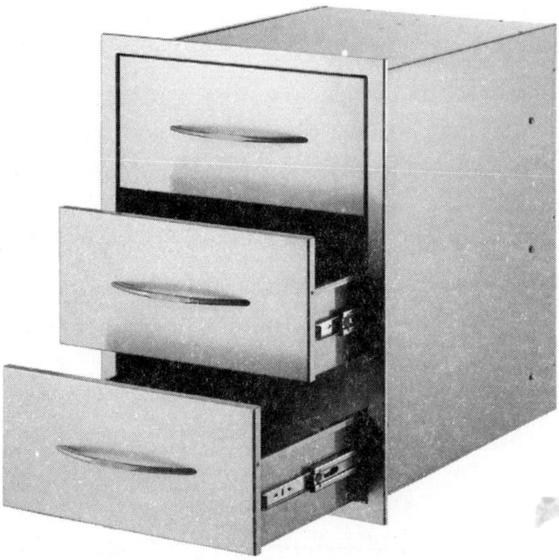

between the objects. The drawers for coins are arranged with slots in them. Cabinets are also used for two-dimensional and three-dimensional objects.

Sliding Screens

Sliding screens are very common for flat works and occasionally for decorative arts, which can be suspended by appropriate hooks. Such system is economical of floor space and is worthwhile for examination and retrieval purposes.

Compaction Devices

Compaction device is fairly recent in the museum world and is the answers for the requirements of more storage and less space. Compaction equipment is intended primarily for permanent storage. The compaction units are operated either electrically or manually. The manual type of compaction equipment is probably more useful for museum storage, as it is less likely to go wrong. Textiles are normally stored using this device but, metal objects can also be stored with appropriate changes in the device.

Vaults

Vaults and security storage areas are used for extremely valuable objects, e.g. gold and silver coins or other treasures like silver, gold and diamond jewellery.

Conservation Guidelines

1. Storage areas should be maintained clean, and the waste and condemned furniture should not be stacked in the storage.
2. If open storage is maintained, the objects should be covered by polypropylene sheets or bags.
3. In order to avoid wastage of space in the storage as well as to avoid dust, slotted angle shelves should be arranged with different-sized boxes containing objects to fit in the space available.
4. The R.H. (relative humidity) and temperature should be maintained at the optimum level and should be monitored regularly.
5. Light sensitive objects should always be kept closed by screens.
6. When scholars are allowed to study the reserve collection, pencil alone should be allowed for writing.
7. Smoking should never be allowed inside the storage area as it involves fire risk.
8. Open fire should never be used even in the form of lamps as it is a fire hazard.
9. Manuscripts should never be kept near windows as it will attract moisture and dust.
10. Proper padding should be placed under metal manuscripts in order to avoid scratching and to facilitate lifting while handling them.
11. Manuscripts should never be directly placed on the floor.
12. Lead manuscripts should not be stored in wooden

cabinets, but on plastic trays, as volatile acids emanated from wood affect lead coins. If wooden cabinets are used, they should be lacquered or varnished. Fibre glass storages may be used alternatively.

13. It is better to have the conservation laboratory attached to the storage in order to arrest some damages in the manuscripts instantly while avoiding transportation.
14. While arranging for the air-conditioning of the storage place, it should be noted that the air-conditioning system should work for twenty-four hours.
15. Interleaving can be done by acid-free card-boards in order to avoid abrasion. One metal resting on the other create potential difference and thus corrosion will be facilitated.

Metal manuscripts are not easily decayed. But corrosion damages the writings, i.e. the engravings, etc., on these. Therefore, it is better that the environment is kept in the optimum condition. The manuscripts should be digitized indoors so that the inscribed matter will be preserved for posterity. Periodic checking and proper house-keeping help the manuscripts to remain in good condition for a longer period.

Bibliography

1. Agrawal, O.P., *Conservation in the Tropics*, International Centre for Conservation, Rome (1972).
2. Oddy, Andrew, (ed.), *The Art of the Conservator*, British Museum, (1992).
3. Thomson, Garry, *The Museum Environment*, Butterworth-Heinemann (1994).
4. Jeyaraj, V., *Heritage Management*, Government

Museum, Chennai (2005).
5. Stolow, Nathan, *Conservation and Exhibition*, Butterworths (1987).
6. Plenderleith, H.J., and Werner, A.E.A., *Conservation of Antiquities and Works of Art*, Oxford University Press, London (1976).
7. Price, Stanley, N.P., (ed.), *Conservation of Archaeological Excavation*, ICCROM, Rome (1984).
8. Bradley, Susan (ed.), *A Guide to the Storage, Exhibition and Handling of Antiquities, Ethnographic and Pictorial Art*, Department of Conservation, British Museum, London (1993).
9. Goffer, Zvi , *Archaeological Chemistry*, John Wiley and Sons (1980).

Notes on Contributors

Achal Pandya is presently Associate Professor (Conservation) in the Indira Gandhi National Centre for the Arts. He did his Masters and Doctorate in Conservation from National Museum Institute of History of Art, Conservation and Museology. He is working on a number of Research Projects and has contributed many articles on conservation.

B.V. Kharbade is presently Project Officer and Head of Regional Conservation Laboratory, Mysore, (A unit of National Research Laboratory for conservation of Cultural Property). He is a Conservation Scientist and has made a very significant contribution to research on conservation of manuscripts.

D.D.N. Singh is a scientist and is presently holding the post of Deputy Director in the National Metallurgical Laboratory, Jamshedpur, India. He has bagged many awards, such as Best Scientist for his outstanding contribution on Corrosion of Metals. He is invited as Guest Speaker by various Universities of U.K. and U.S.A. He has published more than hundred articles in various Research Journals and Seminar Proceedings.

D.G. Suryawanshi is currently the Senior Scientific Officer in NRLC, Lucknow and looks after 'Paper Conservation Research and Training Division'. As a UNESCO Fellow, he went to Italy and did research on 'Evaluation and Testing of changed Products of Paper'. He has conducted a number of conservation training courses for librarians all over the country and delivered lectures in seminars and workshops. Dr. Suryawanshi has published many research articles in National and International Journals.

K.K. Gupta, an expert in the field of conservation was Consultant (Conservation) with IGNCA, New Delhi. He was trained in conservation of cultural heritage in Japan under a UNESCO programme. He has worked for over forty years, on the conservation of antiquities and works of art in the National Museum, New Delhi. Mr. Gupta was also the editor of the Journal 'Conservation of Cultural Property in India' for five years. He has written many articles as well as two books entitled 'Restoration of Oil Paintings' and 'Restoration of Indian Miniatures'.

Samiran Boruah is a well-known artist of miniature paintings. At present he is engaged in cataloguing and in creation of miniature painting in the State Museum of Guwahati. Mr. Boruah has an extensive knowledge of Assamese Paintings used in illustrating the manuscripts.

V. Jeyaraj has been involved in the conservation of museum objects since 1978. He headed the Conservation and Research Laboratory, Government Museum, Chennai and is now retired. He was also the President of the Indian Association for the Study of Conservation of Cultural Property, New Delhi.